PAUL DUNN

The Electrician's Blueprint

Navigate, Innovate & Thrive in Your Electrical Career

Copyright © 2024 by Paul Dunn

©2024 by Paul Dunn. All rights reserved. No part of this publication may be reproduced, distributed, or transmitted in any form or by any means, including photocopying, recording, or other electronic or mechanical methods, without the prior written permission of the publisher, except in the case of brief quotations embodied in critical reviews and certain other non-commercial uses permitted by copyright law. For permission requests, write to the publisher, addressed "Attention: Permissions Coordinator," at the address below.

P. D. Electrical Services (SW) Limited, 2b Portland Street, Ilfracombe, EX34 9NL, United Kingdom

Disclaimer: The information provided in this book, "The Electrician's Blueprint: Navigate, Innovate & Thrive in Your Electrical Career," is for general informational purposes only. All information in the book is provided in good faith, however, the author and publisher make no representation or warranty of any kind, express or implied, regarding the accuracy, adequacy, validity, reliability, availability, or completeness of any information in the book. Under no circumstance shall the author or publisher have any liability to you for any loss or damage of any kind incurred as a result of the use of the book or reliance on any information provided in the book. Your use of the book and your reliance on any information in the book is solely at your own risk. This book does not offer financial advice, and the author and publisher are not liable for any financial claims or losses. The readers should consult with a professional where appropriate before taking any actions based upon the content of this book.

First edition

This book was professionally typeset on Reedsy.
Find out more at reedsy.com

Contents

Important – Read Me First	iv
Introduction	ix
Welcome to the Circuit – Life After Apprenticeship	1
Landing Your First Job	16
Mastering the Business of Electricity	30
The Leap to Self-Employment	44
Growing Your Client Base	57
Financial Fluency for Electricians	71
Technology in Electrical Work	86
Ensuring Customer Satisfaction	100
Building a Strong Professional Network	113
Planning for the Future	128
Shaping Your Electrical Future	142

Important - Read Me First

Hi, I'm Paul Dunn, and I'm grateful you took the opportunity to get this book. The world of electrical work is fast-evolving, and mastering it requires more than just technical skills. It demands a deep understanding of navigating, innovating, and thriving in this industry.

With over 20 years of experience in the electrical field and experience of guiding electricians from apprenticeship to full qualification, I've encountered numerous misconceptions and recurring questions. This experience has driven me to compile the insights and strategies in "The Electrician's Blueprint: Navigate, Innovate & Thrive in Your Electrical Career," a guide dedicated to elevating your professional journey. This guide follows on from our earlier guide, which you may have read, "How to Electrify Your Apprenticeship & Power Up Your Career".

After all, maybe you've struggled with the transition from theory to practice, finding the gap between what textbooks teach and what the job demands wider than you expected. This book aims to bridge that divide, offering real-world advice that is often glossed over in formal education.

Maybe you've found yourself overwhelmed by the administrative and business aspects of electrical work. It's one thing to know how to complete an installation and another to effectively manage client relationships, invoice accurately, and maintain profitability.

Or maybe you've even encountered the challenge of keeping up with the rapid technological advancements within the industry. Staying relevant requires continuous learning and adaptation, which can be daunting when you're just getting your footing.

It seems most new electricians become victims of these common pitfalls. The industry, though rewarding, doesn't always prepare you for the realities of running a successful business or staying ahead in technology. It's tough feeling like you're constantly playing catch-up with no clear guidance on how to progress.

Here's what most don't realise: these challenges aren't just bumps in the road; they are actually pivotal learning opportunities that, when navigated correctly, can lead to significant personal and professional growth.

And now with the possibility of emerging technologies and evolving industry standards, the urgency to adapt has never been more critical. This book provides the tools and insights needed to not only keep up but to excel.

It seems most are left in a state of fear—fear of not being good enough, not knowing enough, or not being able to compete. This anxiety can paralyse even the most talented electricians, preventing them from achieving the success they are capable of.

The Electrician's Vicious Cycle

As a newly qualified electrician, you might find yourself ensnared in a relentless and cyclical struggle, commonly experienced by individuals in your position. This painful loop, which we'll refer to as the Electrician's Vicious Cycle, is a series of phases that continuously loop back on themselves, seemingly offering progress and solutions, only to plunge you back into initial frustrations and setbacks. Let's walk through these stages one by one.

Confusion

Perhaps you've just stepped out, certification in hand, ready to take on the world. But then, the first wave hits – confusion. Where do you start? What kind of jobs should you tackle first? This initial confusion isn't just about choosing between residential or commercial, big or small projects; it's about not knowing how deep the waters are until you're drowning. The overwhelming array of choices and lack of clear direction can make you feel like you're fumbling in the dark, trying to piece together a puzzle without seeing the picture on the box.

Overwhelm

Driven by the initial confusion, you plunge into whatever comes your way. Maybe you take on complex jobs too early, or perhaps you undercharge for straightforward tasks because you're unsure of their true value. This phase is characterized by an overwhelming feeling that there's too much to learn and not enough time to master it all. Each job feels like a test, where the stakes are perpetually high, and every small mistake is amplified.

Frustration

As the reality of your situation sinks in, frustration begins to build. Why aren't things getting easier? You've been working hard, yet every new job seems to bring more challenges than the last. Maybe your clients question your expertise or your ability to manage projects smoothly. This frustration can make you question your decision to become an electrician, as the dream of a thriving career seems to slip through your fingers like sand.

False Confidence

Eventually, a few successes come your way. You complete a couple of jobs with minimal issues, receive good feedback, maybe even start feeling like you've finally cracked the code. This is the stage of false confidence. It's dangerously seductive because it masks the underlying issues that have not been addressed. You might think you've mastered the intricacies of electrical work and running a business, but this phase is merely the calm before the storm.

Disillusionment

And then, the cycle loops back as disillusionment sets in. That big project you thought you handled well? Maybe it returns with complaints about malfunctions or failures. The business practices you thought were solid? Perhaps they aren't as robust as you believed. Suddenly, you find yourself back at square one, facing the same confusion and doubts that plagued you at the start.

It just goes to show that doing something different to gain a better understanding of your work and to become more equipped to handle various projects is essential to break out of this painful cycle. Adopting new strategies and seeking genuine insight into both the technical and business aspects of your career is critical.

Which is why I'm glad you're reading this book, because as you turn the page and start reading, you will finally discover the answers and insight that you've been searching for.

Introduction

Imagine the first day you stepped into your apprenticeship: the smell of new wire, the buzz of current flowing through a system, and that gut-level thrill of creating something functional and critical from mere components. Now fast forward to today. You've mastered the basics, survived the grueling hours of on-the-job training, and passed your exams. Congratulations, you're officially a certified electrician. But, what comes next?

You're standing at the threshold of a career that can be as electrifying as it is daunting. This isn't just about joining the ranks; it's about redefining them. In the world of electrical work, you are now poised to navigate complexities, innovate solutions, and thrive in a landscape that evolves as rapidly as the technologies it depends on. This book is your guide through that journey.

Navigating the New Terrain

Stepping out of apprenticeship and into the field, you might feel like you've got a solid grasp of the technicalities but are less sure about the terrain. It's one thing to know how to wire a complex circuit under supervision, and quite another to tackle unexpected challenges solo or explain issues to a client. This phase of your career is about translating skills into practice and theory into action.

As you embark on this journey, remember that every master electrician started exactly where you are now. They had their first day, their first solo job, and their first big mistake. The key is not just to anticipate the path but to prepare to forge your own. This isn't about avoiding mistakes—it's about learning how to handle them with confidence and expertise.

Innovating Your Approach

Innovation isn't just for tech giants and creative industries. As an electrician, your ability to think outside the fuse box can set you apart from the crowd. This is about more than just following wiring diagrams and safety protocols; it's about seeing the potential for improvements, whether in the energy efficiency of a home or the productivity of a major industrial project.

Your new ideas could lead to better ways of managing projects, solving client problems, or using emerging technologies. Think about smart homes, renewable energy technologies, or advanced automation systems. These arenas offer vast new territories for exploration and expertise. Becoming proficient here not only increases your value as an electrician but also makes you a pivotal player in shaping future landscapes.

Thriving in a Competitive Field

Thriving in your electrical career doesn't necessarily mean being the best sparky on the block. Instead, it's about carving out a niche where you can continuously learn and grow. It's about finding what makes you excited to get up in the morning—whether it's the challenge of a complex industrial installation or the satisfaction of helping a homeowner save energy.

Moreover, thriving means securing your financial future. Understanding the business side of being an electrician—how to manage your accounts, price your services, and communicate with clients—can make the difference between merely getting by and truly prospering. It's also about knowing when to leap into self-employment, how to grow your client base, and how to leverage technology to streamline your workflow and expand your capabilities.

As you move forward, remember that your career is about more than wires and circuits; it's about people. From the clients you advise to the peers you network with, building strong, positive relationships is crucial. Your professional network can support you through downturns, connect you with opportunities, and provide advice when you face tough challenges.

Conclusion

The chapters that follow are designed not just to guide but to inspire. They are filled with practical advice, strategic insights, and real-life examples that will help you navigate the complexities of your career, innovate with confidence, and build a thriving business.

Whether you dream of becoming a go-to expert in renewable energy systems or envision running your own successful contracting business, the journey ahead is ripe with potential. It's time to take everything you've learned so far and build on it, pushing past boundaries, exceeding expectations, and achieving not just competence but excellence.

Welcome to your blueprint for success. Let's get started.

Welcome to the Circuit - Life After Apprenticeship

"Opportunity is missed by most people because it is dressed in overalls and looks like work." - Thomas Edison

Decoding the Electrician's Landscape

Stepping into the electrician's world after your apprenticeship feels a bit like being handed the keys to a complex, powerful machine. You know it works; you've seen it in action, and now it's your turn to drive. But where to start? Let's break down the landscape of the electrical industry, focusing on the current market trends and key players in the UK, so you can navigate this terrain with confidence.

Industry Overview

The UK's electrical sector is a powerhouse, figuratively and literally. It's part of the broader construction industry, but with its own unique dynamics and demands. As a newly qualified electrician, you're entering a field that contributes billions to the UK economy each year. It's a sector that not only powers homes and businesses but also fuels innovations in many other sectors such as technology, manufacturing, and even healthcare.

Electricians are essential, and the demand for skilled professionals like you is robust. From residential installations and maintenance to large-scale industrial projects, the opportunities are vast. The industry is also at the forefront of many green initiatives, with a growing focus on sustainable and renewable energy sources. This means that alongside traditional electrical skills, there's a rising demand for electricians skilled in solar panel installations, wind turbines, and energy-efficient systems.

Current Market Trends

Understanding the trends that shape your industry can give you a competitive edge, so let's plug into the current market currents. The UK electrical sector is seeing significant growth in several key areas:

1. **Smart Home Technology**: With more people automating their homes for efficiency and comfort, skills in integrating and maintaining smart home technology are increasingly valuable. This includes everything from smart meters to home energy management systems that can be controlled via smartphones.

2. **Electric Vehicles (EVs)**: The surge in electric vehicle ownership in the UK has sparked a corresponding demand for public and private charging infrastructure. Installation and maintenance of EV charging stations offer a growing niche for electricians.

3. **Regulation and Compliance**: With the government tightening regulations on safety and energy efficiency, there's a heightened need for compliance. This means more work in ensuring existing installations meet the latest standards, and new installations are up to code.

4. **Renewable Energy Systems**: As mentioned, the shift towards renewables is creating more opportunities. Whether it's solar, wind, or geothermal systems, having expertise in these areas can set you apart.

5. **Retrofitting and Upgrades**: The UK's ageing infrastructure means there's plenty of work in updating old systems. This includes retrofitting buildings with new wiring, lighting, and energy-efficient technologies.

By keeping your finger on the pulse of these trends, you can better position yourself as a specialist and capitalize on the areas of highest demand.

Key Players in the UK Electrical Sector

Knowing who the key players are can help you understand the ecosystem you're operating in. It's also useful for networking and career advancement. The landscape includes a mix of large multinational corporations, mid-sized companies, and small firms, along with various suppliers, regulatory bodies, and trade associations.

Major Companies: Companies like Siemens, Schneider Electric, and ABB are big names in the industry, involved in everything from manufacturing electrical components to complex systems integration and consulting.

Trade Associations: The Electrical Contractors' Association (ECA) and SELECT are crucial for advocacy, training, and standards. Membership in such bodies can enhance your credibility and provide valuable networking opportunities.

Regulatory Bodies: The Institution of Engineering and Technology (IET) sets standards in electrical and electronic engineering, while the Health and Safety Executive (HSE) oversees safety compliance in the workplace.

Educational Institutions: Universities and colleges play a key role in research and training. Keeping an eye on their programmes and partnerships can provide insights into emerging technologies and skills demands.

Navigating this landscape involves understanding both the

opportunities and the requirements of your new role. By staying informed about industry trends, key players, and the overall market dynamics, you equip yourself not just to participate but to excel. As you move forward, remember that each connection, project, and learning opportunity helps to wire your career for success.

Tools of the Trade

Embarking on your journey as a newly qualified electrician, you're about to discover that your tools aren't just accessories; they are your allies. Understanding what to include in your toolkit, how to maintain these crucial items, and when to invest in more advanced instruments will set the foundation for your success and safety in this dynamic field.

Essential Tools for a Newly Qualified Electrician

As you step into the electrical trade, the array of tools available might seem overwhelming. However, focusing on the essentials can streamline your transition from an apprentice to a proficient electrician. Start with these must-haves:

1. **Multimeter**: This is your best friend in the field. A reliable multimeter can measure voltage, current, and resistance, which are fundamental for diagnosing electrical problems efficiently

2. **Wire Strippers**: Precision is key in electrical work, and a durable pair of wire strippers will provide you with the accuracy needed for stripping and cutting wires without damaging them

3. **Screwdrivers and Nut Drivers**: Invest in a set that includes various sizes and types, particularly those insulated for electrical work to protect you against electric shocks.

4. **Pliers**: Needle-nose pliers, side-cutting pliers, and tongue-and-groove pliers are essential for gripping, twisting, cutting, and pulling wires.

5. **Voltage Tester**: Before you manipulate any wiring, checking for live currents is crucial. A non-contact voltage tester offers a quick and safe way to perform these checks.

6. **Tape Measure**: Whether it's measuring for conduit runs or spacing out light fixtures, a sturdy tape measure is indispensable.

7. **Fish Tape**: For pulling wire through conduit or in tight spaces, a fish tape is essential. It's your go-to tool for navigating wires through complex routes.

8. **Torpedo Level**: Precision isn't just about measurement; ensuring your installations are perfectly level can prevent future issues and callbacks.

9. **Flashlight or Headlamp**: Adequate lighting is non-negotiable when working with electricity. Opt for a durable, high-lumen flashlight or a hands-free headlamp.

10. **Tool Belt or Bag**: Keeping all your tools easily accessible and organised is vital. A robust tool belt or a spacious tool bag will save you time and frustration on the job.

Each of these tools serves a distinct purpose, aiding your daily tasks and ensuring your work not only meets but exceeds expectations.

Maintaining Your Toolkit

Tool maintenance might not be the most glamorous part of your job, but it's absolutely essential. Well-maintained tools perform better, last longer, and most importantly, keep you safe. Here's how to keep your toolkit in top shape:

Regular Cleaning: Dust, debris, and other contaminants can wear out your tools. Wipe them down after each use and store them in a clean, dry place

Inspection: Before use, inspect each tool for damage such as cracked handles, worn out grips, or loose components. Damaged tools are not just inefficient, they're dangerous.

Lubrication: Tools with moving parts, like pliers, require occasional lubrication to keep them operating smoothly.

Sharpening: Keep cutting tools like wire strippers sharp; dull tools require more force to use, which increases the risk of accidents.

Electrical Checks: For powered tools, regularly check cords and batteries. Frayed cords and weak batteries can affect the performance of your tools and pose safety risks.

Professional Servicing: Some tools will occasionally need professional attention. This is particularly true for high-precision instruments like multimeters. Testers will require regular calibration to ensure accuracy.

Advanced Tools Investment

As your career progresses, you'll encounter situations that demand more sophisticated technology. Investing in advanced tools can enhance your efficiency, accuracy, and service quality. Consider these additions:

1. **Circuit Finder**: Ideal for complex circuits or renovations, a circuit finder can save you considerable time and effort in identifying circuits at the breaker box.

2. **Thermal Imaging Camera**: For diagnosing issues like overheating and energy loss without contact, a thermal imaging camera is invaluable. It's a significant investment but can set you apart in terms of service delivery.

3. **Oscilloscope**: When you need to observe the precise waveforms of electrical signals, an oscilloscope can provide insights that basic tools cannot.

4. **Ground Resistance Tester**: This tool is crucial for verifying the safety and effectiveness of grounding systems, an essential

check in both residential and commercial settings.

While these tools represent a considerable investment, they are worth considering as you build a reputation for thorough, professional, and high-quality electrical work. Each tool not only adds a layer of efficiency and safety to your operations but also enhances your ability to tackle more complex and lucrative projects.

Navigating through your tool needs as a newly qualified electrician sets the stage for a flourishing career. From the basics that form the backbone of your daily operations to advanced equipment that pushes the boundaries of what you can offer, each tool you select is a step forward in your professional journey. Remember, the right tools not only make a job possible; they make it easier and safer, allowing you to deliver your best work confidently and competently.

Safety First

Navigating the electrician's landscape with skill and precision is one thing, but keeping safety at the forefront is quite another and arguably more crucial. As a newly qualified electrician, you're stepping into a world where the stakes are high, and the margin for error is slim. Let's dive into the essentials of safety you need to embrace from day one.

Understanding UK Electrical Safety Standards

You might have come across the term "BS7671" during your training days. This is the national standard for electrical installations in the UK, and it's your new bible. Familiarizing yourself with the BS7671, also known as the Wiring Regulations, is not just about compliance—it's about ensuring that every wire you connect, every circuit you complete, is done in the safest way possible.

These regulations are updated regularly to reflect new technologies and safer practices, so keeping your knowledge up-to-date is a continuous process. One effective way to stay informed is by subscribing to updates from the Institution of Engineering and Technology (IET) and attending their seminars and workshops. This proactive approach will not only keep you safe but also elevate your professional reputation.

Another key standard is the Electricity at Work Regulations 1989, which outlines the responsibilities of employers and employees in maintaining safety standards at work. Understanding these regulations will guide you on how to handle electrical systems safely, protecting not just yourself but also your colleagues and clients.

Remember, understanding these standards isn't just about avoiding legal repercussions; it's more fundamentally about creating a safe working environment. Every regulation is designed with human safety in mind, reflecting lessons learned from past incidents. Treat them as wisdom passed down to save lives, including potentially your own.

Risk Assessment Basics

Now, let's talk risk assessment. This isn't just a box-ticking exercise. It's a fundamental skill that could be the difference between a regular day at work and a catastrophic one. Conducting a thorough risk assessment before beginning any electrical task is not just good practice—it's essential.

Start by identifying potential hazards. In the electrical world, these could range from exposed wires and overloaded circuits to working at height or in confined spaces. Once you've identified these hazards, evaluate the risk associated with each. Ask yourself questions like: How likely is it that this hazard could cause harm? And if it does, how severe could the consequences be?

After evaluating the risks, it's time to decide on precautions. Can you eliminate the hazard entirely? If not, how can you control the risk so that harm is unlikely? This might include measures such as using insulated tools, wearing appropriate personal protective equipment, or implementing additional safety checks.

Documenting your risk assessments is also vital. Not only does it provide a record that you've addressed potential hazards, but it also helps in continually improving safety practices. Over time, you'll be able to look back on past assessments and adjust your approach based on what has worked (or not).

Personal Protective Equipment

Last but by no means least, let's gear up—literally. Personal Protective Equipment (PPE) is your last line of defence against on-site hazards, and skimping on it isn't an option. At a basic level, you'll need hard-wearing gloves to protect against cuts and burns, safety goggles for eye protection, and ear defenders in environments with high noise levels. Each piece of PPE has its own specific context and standards; for instance, gloves insulated against electrical shocks are a must when working with live circuits.

Your footwear also matters more than you might think. Insulated boots can prevent life-threatening electrical shocks, and sturdy, slip-resistant soles can avert falls from ladders or wet surfaces. Helmets might not always be fashionable, but they can save your life, protecting against both falling objects and accidental head contact with electrical hazards.

In the realm of electrical work, where the risk of arc flashes exists, flame-resistant clothing becomes essential. These specially designed garments can help mitigate the severity of burns in case of an electrical explosion. Remember, PPE is not just equipment but a vital investment in your safety.

It's crucial to maintain your Paddle with the same diligence you apply to your tools. Regular checks and maintenance ensure that your gear provides maximum protection. Look for signs of wear and tear, particularly in items regularly exposed to harsh conditions, like gloves and helmets. Replace any item that shows signs of damage or deterioration; it's a small expense compared to the cost of injury.

As a newly qualified electrician, entering the field might feel like stepping into a live circuit—thrilling, but fraught with potential dangers. However, arming yourself with knowledge of safety standards, practicing thorough risk assessments, and investing in and maintaining quality Paddle not only ensures your safety but also elevates the quality of your work and your reputation in this critical field. Remember, in electrical work, safety is not just a regulation; it's a lifestyle.

Recap & Action Items

You've just powered through a comprehensive guide that's set to illuminate your path in the electrical industry. From understanding the ever-evolving landscape of the sector to equipping yourself with the right tools and prioritising safety, you're now better prepared to thrive as a newly qualified electrician.

Firstly, reflect on the current market trends and key players in the UK electrical sector you've learnt about. This isn't just trivia; it's the GPS map for your career journey. Identify companies or industry leaders you admire and consider how you might align yourself with the types of innovations and practices they champion.

Now, let's talk toolkit. You've got a rundown of the essential tools every electrician should own. If you haven't yet, start investing in these tools. Remember, quality over quantity. It's better to have a few reliable tools that won't fail you than a box full of second-rate equipment. Gradually expand your toolkit as your skills and budget allow. Keep an eye on those advanced tools you'll eventually need; planning your investments in these can really set you apart from the competition.

Safety can never be overstressed. Make it your mantra to review the UK electrical safety standards regularly. These aren't just guidelines; they're your lifeline. Practise risk assessments diligently, even when it feels like second nature. Always wear and maintain your personal protective equipment, no matter how small the job. Safety is what ensures that at the end of the day, you go home healthy.

Here are your action steps:

1. **Map Out Key Players**: Create a list of companies and leaders in the industry whose values align with yours. Research their work, follow them on professional networks, and stay updated with their innovations

2. **Tool Acquisition Plan**: Draft a budget for your toolkit essentials and future investments. Prioritise tools based on your immediate needs and typical job demands.

3. **Safety Routine Check**: Develop a routine to check and

maintain your safety gear. Integrate regular reviews of safety standards into your weekly schedule to ensure you're always ahead of the curve.

By taking these steps, you're not just working on jobs; you're building a career. Welcome to the circuit – it's time to make your mark!

Landing Your First Job

"Opportunities don't happen, you create them." - Chris Grosser

Crafting a Winning CV

Embarking on a new career is akin to setting up a sophisticated circuit - every connection must be precise to ensure the whole system functions seamlessly. Your CV is the initial spark in your job application process; it's what lights up your chances to stand out in the competitive field of electrical engineering. Let's break down the essentials to craft a CV that not only ticks all the boxes but also flips the right switches for potential employers.

What Employers are Looking For

First things first, understanding the landscape of employer expectations in the electrical industry is crucial. It's not just about listing your qualifications and experiences; it's about presenting them in a way that resonates with the needs and values of your prospective employer. Most employers are on the lookout for a few key elements:

1. **Relevant Qualifications**: This includes both your educational background and any certifications pertinent to the field of electrical work, such as an NVQ Level 3 Diploma in Electrotechnical Services. It's essential to list these qualifications upfront and clearly.

2. **Practical Experience**: Whether it's an apprenticeship, placements, or part-time work, real-world experience counts. Employers want to see that you've applied your theoretical knowledge in practical settings, tackling real problems and finding effective solutions.

3. **Technical Skills**: From understanding wiring regulations to proficiency in using CAD software for designing electrical systems, highlight the specific technical skills that align with the job you are applying for.

4. **Soft Skills**: Communication, problem-solving, and teamwork are just as crucial in an electrician's role as technical expertise. Electrical projects often require collaboration, so demonstrating that you can work effectively with others is a significant plus.

5. **Attention to Detail and Safety Awareness**: Given the high stakes involved in electrical work, employers prioritise candidates who showcase a meticulous approach to safety and regulations.

Tailoring Your CV to Electrical Jobs

Now that you've got a grasp on what's expected, let's tailor your CV to reflect these needs. Each job application should be customised — think of it as rewiring a circuit each time to optimise performance.

Personalise Your Objective Statement: Start with a strong, specific objective that aligns with the job role. For instance, "Seeking to leverage my two-year apprenticeship experience and NVQ Level 3 Diploma in Electrotechnical Services to contribute to the innovative projects at XYZ Electricals."

Highlight Relevant Experience: List your experiences in reverse chronological order, emphasising those most relevant to electrical work. Use bullet points to describe your responsibilities and achievements in each role, quantifying results whenever possible (e.g., "Reduced wiring time by 20% through streamlined processes").

Showcase Your Projects: If you've worked on any notable projects during your apprenticeship or previous employment, detail these separately. Describe the project, your role, and any recognition you received as a result.

Skill Section is Vital: Create a separate section for technical skills and software proficiencies. Also, include a subsection for soft skills, linking them to real-life applications (e.g., "Enhanced team communication, leading to a 30% reduction in project errors").

Include Additional Information: If you've attended workshops or taken extra courses relevant to the electrical industry, list them. Also, memberships in professional bodies like the Institution of Engineering and Technology (IET) can be a significant boost.

Highlighting Apprenticeship Experience

Apprenticeships are golden tickets in your CV, especially when you're kickstarting your career. They demonstrate not only your capability to learn and adapt but also your commitment to the profession.

Detail Your Learning: Describe the scope of your apprenticeship — what skills did you acquire? What type of projects did you handle? How did this experience prepare you for a full-time role? Be specific.

Mention Mentoring: Talk about working with experienced electricians and how this mentorship helped you grow professionally. This not only shows that you've been trained by skilled professionals but also that you value learning and development.

Quantify Achievements: If you can, quantify your contributions during your apprenticeship. Did you increase efficiency? Reduce costs? Solve a particularly challenging problem? Numbers speak louder than words.

Your CV is more than a document; it's a testament to your

readiness to enter and thrive in the electrical field. By aligning it closely with what employers are looking for, tailoring it to specific job descriptions, and effectively highlighting your apprenticeship experience, you set the stage not just to land an interview, but to electrify your entire career path.

Acing the Interview

Common Interview Questions

Stepping into your first job interview in the electrical industry can feel like facing the final boss in a video game: daunting but definitely doable with the right strategies. To begin with, understanding the typical questions you might encounter will give you a solid foundation. Remember, most employers are not just assessing your technical know-how; they're keen to grasp your problem-solving skills, your ability to work under pressure, and how well you mesh with a team.

So, first up, expect the basics like, "Tell me about yourself." It's a soft pitch, but don't be fooled into thinking it's trivial. Here, you're not just recounting your life story. Tailor your response to highlight aspects of your background that align with being a reliable, skilled electrician. Perhaps mention the hands-on projects during your apprenticeship or the extra courses you took to better understand electrical codes.

Then there's the inevitable, "Why do you want to work here?"

Before the interview, do your homework on the company. Are they innovators in renewable energy installations? Do they have a sterling reputation for customer service? Whatever the hook, let them know that their company's ethos resonates with your professional values and ambitions.

Technical questions will vary widely, but you might get scenarios to solve, such as, "How would you address a sudden power outage during a project?" Here, they're watching for your practical knowledge as well as your ability to communicate effectively and calmly. Outline your step-by-step approach to diagnosing and solving the issue, emphasising safety and efficiency.

Lastly, prepare for behavioural questions aimed at uncovering how you handle situations. "Tell me about a time when you had to work under tight deadlines." Use the STAR method (Situation, Task, Action, Result) to structure your answers, showing your thought process and initiative in resolving challenges.

Demonstrating Practical Knowledge

In the world of electrical work, showing what you know is just as crucial as talking about it. When an interviewer asks a technical question, view it as your stage to shine. For instance, if asked to explain how you would perform a specific installation or repair, don't just dive into the technical jargon. Start by explaining the safety checks you would perform. This not only shows your competency but also that you prioritise safety, a huge plus in this field.

If possible, bring along a portfolio of your work. This could include diagrams of circuits you've designed or photos of completed projects. It's one thing to say you've installed complex wiring systems; it's another to show a neatly organised fuse box you wired up.

During some interviews, especially for hands-on roles, you might even be given a practical test. This could range from identifying tools based on their function, to actually performing a task like wiring a plug. Prior practice is crucial here. Spend time in a workshop setting (safely, of course) refining your techniques so that when it comes to demonstrating your skills under observation, you're ready and confident.

Interview Etiquette in the Electrical Industry

Navigating interview etiquette in the electrical industry isn't massively different from other fields, but there are nuances. For starters, dress appropriately. While you might be used to the work boots and tool belt, an interview usually calls for a neat, professional look. Think clean, pressed trousers and a button-down shirt. It shows respect and effort.

Punctuality is non-negotiable. Arriving even five minutes late can send the wrong signal. It's not just about respecting the interviewer's time; it's about proving you can manage your own effectively — a must for any electrician who will be juggling multiple clients and sites.

During the interview, be mindful of your body language. Maintain eye contact, offer a firm handshake, and sit upright. These are universal signs of confidence and respect. Listen attentively and answer questions clearly and concisely. Rambling is a common nervous response but try to keep your answers focused and on point.

Remember to turn off your phone before the interview begins. It's a small gesture, but it shows you're fully present and not about to be distracted by a call about another job or a text.

Lastly, the electrical industry thrives on precision and attention to detail. Reflect these qualities in how you present yourself and respond to questions. Every little aspect of your interaction should communicate that you are meticulous and thorough — key traits of a top-notch electrician.

By preparing thoroughly, demonstrating your knowledge confidently, and observing the right etiquette, you're setting yourself up not just to ace the interview but to electrify your career path right from the start.

Securing the Position

After you've impressed with your CV and aced your interview, you might think the hardest part is over. But don't kick back just yet; the game isn't over until you've officially landed the job. This final stretch is about keeping the momentum going and crossing that finish line. Here's how you can secure your position, negotiate your salary, and start your electrical career on the right foot.

Follow-up Strategies

So, you've left the interview room with a handshake and a smile, what's next? The key now is to remain on the radar without coming off as pushy. It's a delicate balance, but get it right, and you're in a strong position to grab that job offer.

First thing's first: send a thank-you email. This should be done within24 hours of your interview. It's not just about showing you have good manners; it's about reinforcing a positive impression. Make your email brief but impactful. Thank the interviewer for their time, reiterate your enthusiasm for the role, and why you think you're a good fit. This is your chance to touch on a high point from the interview, something that you connected on, or a shared value or enthusiasm.

Next, if you haven't heard back within the timeframe they indicated, it's acceptable to send a follow-up email. Keep it professional and courteous. Express your continued interest in the position and inquire if any further information on your part is needed. If you still don't hear back, a final follow-up after another week is acceptable. Beyond this, it's best to hold tight and avoid the risk of appearing desperate.

What if the response is a 'no'? Use it as an opportunity. Ask for feedback on your interview and what you might improve. This shows professionalism and dedication to your personal growth, leaving a positive lasting impression that could be beneficial for future opportunities.

Negotiating Your Salary

Congratulations, you've got a job offer! But before you rush to accept, let's talk about the salary. It's perfectly normal to discuss your salary and, done right, can show that you value yourself and your skills.

Before you enter negotiations, do your homework. Research typical salaries for the position in your area. Websites like Glassdoor, PayScale, and indeed can provide you with a ballpark figure. This will give you the confidence to discuss numbers and the evidence to back up your request.

When the topic comes up, be honest but also be realistic. Express appreciation for the offer and then present your case. Perhaps you have unique skills or certifications that are advantageous to the job, or maybe your apprenticeship experience gives you a head start that can benefit your employer. Use these as leverage.

Remember, salary isn't the only negotiable aspect of your job offer. Consider other benefits such as vacation time, flexible working hours, professional development opportunities, or even a signing bonus. Sometimes these can be just as valuable as the salary itself.

If the employer can't meet your salary expectations, consider whether the job may offer other forms of value like professional growth, a stepping stone into the industry, or exceptional work-life balance. Sometimes these factors may justify a lower initial offer.

Starting on the Right Foot

You've signed the contract, and now it's time to show you're as good as they believed you to be. First impressions count, so make your first day count. Dress appropriately, arrive early, and come prepared to learn and to contribute.

Take initiative right from the start. Be proactive about introducing yourself to your new colleagues and learning the ropes. Show interest in the broader aspects of the company, not just your specific role. This shows that you are keen and ready to be a part of the team.

Keep a keen attitude towards continuous learning. The electrical industry is ever-evolving with new technologies and regulations. Showing a willingness to stay updated and adapt is crucial. Ask questions, seek feedback, and demonstrate that you're not just there to do a job, but to excel and grow.

Remember, the initial weeks in any job can be challenging. You're learning a lot, not just about your job but also about the culture and dynamics of the workplace. Be patient with yourself but stay enthusiastic and committed. It's this blend of eagerness and perseverance that will set you apart as a valuable member of the team.

In summary, securing your position in the electrical career field doesn't end at the interview. Following up effectively, negotiating your salary wisely, and starting your new role with enthusiasm and professionalism are all crucial steps to ensure your long-term success and satisfaction in your new job. So, take these steps seriously, and you'll not only secure your position but also pave the way for a promising career ahead.

Recap & Action Items

Congratulations! You've just equipped yourself with the essential tools to kickstart your career in the electrical industry. Let's do a quick recap and set some actionable steps to ensure you hit the ground running.

Firstly, your CV is your first impression. Remember, it's not just about listing your experiences; it's about presenting them in a way that resonates with what employers in the electrical field are looking for. Tailor your CV to highlight your technical skills and any apprenticeship experience, making sure to emphasise your hands-on capabilities and any real-world applications of your skills.

Next, mastering the interview is crucial. You now know the

common questions to expect and how to demonstrate your practical knowledge effectively. Always keep in mind the unique etiquette expected in the electrical industry; be punctual, present yourself professionally, and show that you're ready to be a part of a practical, hands-on world.

Finally, securing the position extends beyond just performing well in the interview. Follow up with a thank-you note to express your appreciation for the opportunity and reaffirm your interest in the role. If an offer is made, don't shy away from negotiating your salary. Remember, this is a practice that can set the tone for your earnings and benefits throughout your career. Start on the right foot by understanding your worth and the value you bring to the company.

Action Steps:

1. Update your CV this week. Use the guidelines provided to align it closely with industry expectations

2. Prepare answers to common interview questions and rehearse them with a friend or mentor who can provide feedback

3. Create a follow-up email template that you can customise after each interview

4. Research salary ranges for entry-level electricians in your area to help during negotiations

5. Reflect on every interview to continually refine and improve your approach.

By taking these steps, you'll not only prepare yourself to land your first job in the electrical industry but also set a strong foundation for a thriving career. Keep learning, stay adaptable, and always be ready to showcase your skills and passion.

Mastering the Business of Electricity

"Success in management requires learning as fast as the world is changing." - Warren Bennis

Understanding Contract Work

Navigating the complex world of electrical contracts is a bit like trying to solve a Rubik's Cube in the dark. It's tricky, but with the right tools and some illumination, you can crack it. Whether you're just starting out or looking to refine your expertise, mastering contract work is fundamental to thriving in your electrical career. Let's break down this puzzle into manageable parts, starting with the types of electrical contracts, moving through how to interpret these documents, and finishing off with tips to sidestep common pitfalls.

Types of Electrical Contracts

As you dive into the electrical industry, you'll encounter several types of contracts. Understanding the nuances of each is crucial for managing expectations, both yours and your clients'.

1. **Fixed-Price Contracts**: These are the bread and butter of electrical contracts where you agree to complete specified work for a set price. It sounds straightforward, but the devil is in the details. Ensure that the scope of the work is crystal clear to avoid scope creep, which can eat into your profits.

2. **Cost-Plus Contracts**: Here, the client agrees to pay the costs of the project plus a fee, which could be a fixed amount or a percentage of the costs. These contracts can be a bit of a tightrope as they require meticulous record-keeping to justify the costs.

3. **Time and Materials Contracts (T&M)**: In these agreements, your client pays for the time spent and materials used. They offer flexibility but require a high level of trust from clients, as they can see costs mount if the project encounters hurdles.

4. **Unit Pricing Contracts**: Common in larger projects, these contracts charge per unit installed, which can be great if you have a good handle on your unit costs but risky if unexpected issues arise that increase installation time or material costs.

Each type of contract has its place, and choosing the right one depends on the project size, the clarity of the requirements, and how much risk you're willing to take on. As a rule of thumb, the more uncertain a project, the more cautious you should be about fixed-price contracts.

Reading and Understanding Contracts

Think of a contract as a roadmap. It doesn't just tell you the destination but also the routes and potential roadblocks. Here's how to navigate this map:

Clarity is King: Look for clear, concise language. If something isn't clear, it's a breeding ground for disputes. Don't be shy to ask for clarifications or adjustments before signing.

Scope of Work: This section is the heartbeat of your contract. It tells you what's expected on both sides. Make sure every task you are to perform is outlined. If it's not included and you think it should be, get it in there before you agree to anything.

Payment Terms: Know when and how you will be paid, and what happens if a payment is late. This affects your cash flow, so it's more important than it might seem at first glance.

Liabilities and Warranties: Understand what you are liable for and what you are warranting in your work. This can protect you from unfair claims but can also commit you to extensive rectifications if things go wrong.

Termination Clauses: No one likes to think about breaking up before even getting together, but understanding how either party can terminate the contract is crucial. It can save you from being stuck in an unprofitable or frustrating project.

Avoiding Common Contractual Pitfalls

Now for the booby traps. Here are common pitfalls you can easily avoid with a bit of foresight:

1. **Over-committing**: Don't let enthusiasm or eagerness for new business lead you to agree to unrealistic timelines or deliverables. Over-committing can strain your resources and harm your reputation.

2. **Vague Terms**: Ambiguity is the mother of dispute. Ensure all terms, especially those regarding scope of work and payment, are as specific as possible.

3. **Ignoring the Fine Print**: Sometimes, key obligations or restrictions are buried in the fine print. Take your time to read through every part of the contract, no matter how tedious it seems.

4. **Skipping Legal Review**: Especially when you're new, having a legal expert review your contracts can save you from costly mistakes. Consider it an investment in your business's health.

5. **Failing to Plan for Disputes**: Include a dispute resolution clause in your contracts. Decide whether arbitration or media-

tion could be alternatives to court, which can be expensive and time-consuming.

By understanding the different types of contracts, knowing how to read and interpret these documents effectively, and being aware of common pitfalls, you can set a solid foundation for success in your electrical projects. Remember, every contract is a step towards building your reputation and your business. Handle them wisely, and they'll lead you to a thriving career in the electrifying world of electricity.

Effective Communication

In the electrifying world of electrical work, the voltage of your technical skills matters, but your capacity to communicate effectively can truly amp up your career. Let's dive into the circuitry of communication within the electrical industry, focusing on how to connect with clients and contractors, manage tough talks, and keep your documentation and reporting crystal clear.

Communicating with Clients and Contractors

Imagine you're at a bustling job site. The hum of machinery is in the background, sparks occasionally fly – it's your arena. Here, every interaction can lead to new opportunities or could trip the breaker on potential deals. Communicating effectively isn't just about talking; it's about engaging in a way that resonates and builds trust.

Firstly, know your audience. Your client might not understand the technical jargon that rolls off your tongue. Phrases like 'circuit load' or 'service upgrade' could be foreign terms to them. Simplify your language without diluting the information. For instance, instead of saying, "We need a 20-amp circuit," you might say, "We need to upgrade to a safer, more robust system for your new appliances." This not only makes the information more digestible but also highlights the benefits of the work.

Active listening is your best tool. Pay attention to what your clients and contractors are really saying, which often goes beyond words. Are they hesitant or confused? Maybe they need more reassurance or a simpler explanation of the costs and benefits. By acknowledging their concerns and responding appropriately, you build a bridge of trust.

Feedback loops are crucial. Regular updates can preempt confusion and frustration. Whether it's a quick call to confirm a design detail or a weekly email update on project progress, these touchpoints can keep everyone aligned and satisfied.

Lastly, body language speaks volumes. Maintaining eye contact, nodding, and facing the person you are talking to, all signal that you are engaged and respectful. Even on your busiest days, these small gestures can make a big impact.

Handling Difficult Conversations

No matter how well you plan and communicate, you'll inevitably face tough conversations. It could be about project delays, unexpected cost overruns, or dissatisfaction with some aspect of a job. How you handle these talks can define your career.

Always approach with a calm and professional demeanor. Before you dive into the discussion, take a deep breath and remind yourself that the goal is resolution, not escalation. Start by clearly stating what you understand to be the issue. This shows you're informed and attentive.

Empathy is your ally. Acknowledge the other person's feelings and frustrations without immediately jumping in with your solutions or defences. For example, you might say, "I understand why that would be frustrating," before explaining the situation.

Facts are your friends, but keep them clear and straightforward. Prepare the points you need to discuss and avoid overwhelming technical details that might derail the conversation.

Offer solutions or alternatives where possible. People appreciate proactive problem-solving. If a delay is unavoidable, explain why and how you plan to mitigate the impact on the overall project. Maybe you can accelerate another part of the project, or offer a discount on certain services as compensation.

Remember, follow-up after a tough conversation can turn a negative into a positive. A quick call or email to ensure the other party feels heard and valued after the resolution can help maintain and even strengthen business relationships.

Documentation and Reporting

In the realm of electrical work, documentation and reporting are the backbone of professional communication. They ensure that everyone involved in a project is on the same page, and they provide a clear record that can help you manage expectations and protect against liabilities.

Start with clarity in your documentation. Whether it's a project proposal, a progress report, or an invoice, clear and concise documents reduce the chances of misunderstandings. Use headings, bullet points, and diagrams where appropriate to break down complex information into digestible pieces.

Consistency is key. Develop templates for your common documents. This not only saves you time but also ensures that you don't omit crucial information in the hustle of a busy schedule.

Regular reporting keeps clients and contractors informed and engaged. Schedule weekly or bi-weekly updates, depending on the scale of the project, and stick to that timetable. These reports don't have to be exhaustive—a brief overview of what's been completed, what's up next, and any issues encountered will suffice.

Lastly, ensure your documentation is accessible but secure.

Use cloud storage solutions that allow you to share files with stakeholders easily while protecting sensitive information. This approach not only streamlines communication but also adds a layer of professionalism to your operations.

Effective communication in the electrical field is much like wiring a house. Each connection must be precise and purposeful, ensuring that the entire system functions seamlessly. By mastering these skills, you not only illuminate your path but also ensure a brighter career trajectory.

Time Management Mastery

Scheduling and Planning

In the buzzing world of electrical work, the art of scheduling and planning isn't just good practice—it's essential survival gear. You, as a budding electrician, may often find yourself juggling multiple projects, each with its own set of intricate demands and deadlines. Mastering this segment can very well mean the difference between thriving in your career and watching it short-circuit before it even gets going.

To start, embrace the power of digital tools. Whether it's a basic calendar app or more sophisticated project management software, these tools can help you keep track of your projects and deadlines efficiently. Lay out a clear plan at the beginning of each project. This should include a timeline of tasks, required materials, and any dependencies, such as waiting for certain components to arrive or needing a particular area cleared by other contractors before you can begin your work.

Remember, good planning is proactive rather than reactive. Anticipate potential snags and build in buffers. For instance, if you estimate a job will take three days, schedule four. This extra day accounts for unforeseen circumstances like delivery delays or last-minute client changes.

Moreover, review your schedule daily. At the end of each day, spend a few minutes to update your tasks and adjust your plans based on what you accomplished. This will keep you on track and alert you early to any potential delays, allowing you to communicate these in a timely manner to clients or colleagues.

Prioritising Tasks

As you become more entrenched in the electrical field, you'll quickly realise that not all tasks are created equal. Some will be critical to the completion of a project, while others, though necessary, can be deferred. Prioritising tasks effectively ensures that you're always working on the right thing at the right time, maximising productivity and reducing downtime.

Start each day by identifying the tasks that are critical for that day. Use the Eisenhower Box technique to sort your tasks into four categories: urgent and important, important but not urgent, urgent but not important, and neither urgent nor important. Your goal is to focus on tasks that are both urgent and important to keep your projects on track. Tasks that are important but not urgent can be scheduled for later, while those that are urgent but not important can be delegated if possible.

Another handy approach is the ABC method where you assign a priority status of A, B, or C to each task. 'A' tasks are high priority, must-do tasks. 'B' tasks are important but can wait, and 'C' tasks are nice to do but not necessary. Start with your 'A' tasks and don't move on to 'B' or 'C' tasks until the 'A' tasks are completed.

This prioritisation ensures that you manage your energy and focus on the tasks that will drive your projects forward. It also helps in managing the expectations of clients and supervisors, as you'll be tackling the most impactful tasks first.

Dealing with Job Delays and Disruptions

In an ideal world, every job would go exactly to plan. However, in the dynamic field of electrical work, delays and disruptions are not just common; they're part of the daily landscape. Whether it's a delayed shipment of parts, unexpected structural challenges, or last-minute changes requested by a client, your ability to handle these disruptions can set you apart from less adaptable competitors.

Firstly, maintain open lines of communication. When a delay occurs, inform all relevant parties promptly. This includes your team members, project managers, and clients. Explaining the situation and the steps you are taking to mitigate the delay not only manages expectations but also demonstrates your professionalism and commitment to the project.

Next, always have a contingency plan. When planning your projects, think about possible points of failure and develop strategies to address these. If a particular component often experiences shipping delays, consider keeping a small stock on hand or having a secondary supplier you can turn to if needed.

Lastly, use delays as an opportunity to catch up on other tasks. If you're waiting on materials for one project, shift your focus to another where progress can be made. This helps maintain momentum and keeps your overall productivity high.

Effective time management in the electrical trade isn't just about keeping projects on track; it's about building a reputation as reliable, efficient, and supremely capable. By mastering scheduling and planning, prioritising tasks effectively, and managing delays and disruptions adeptly, you set yourself up for a thriving career in this fast-paced industry.

Recap & Action Items

You've just navigated through the essential frameworks of mastering the business side of your electrical career. Let's take a moment to consolidate your gains and prepare you to apply these insights effectively.

First, your understanding of contract work is vital. Remember, every contract you engage with is more than just paper; it's the blueprint of your job responsibilities and expectations. Take the time to thoroughly review each contract, familiarising yourself with common terms and clauses. This will guard you against common pitfalls, such as scope creep or unclear payment terms. Make it a habit to review contracts with a mentor or legal advisor until you feel confident in your understanding.

Next, we tackled effective communication. The ability to clearly convey your thoughts and negotiate with clients and contractors is invaluable. Challenging conversations are part of the job, but handling them with professionalism will set you apart. Always follow up verbal communications with written confirmations to avoid misunderstandings and maintain clarity. Consider role-playing scenarios with a peer to hone your communication skills, particularly in handling objections or negotiating terms.

Lastly, your mastery of time management will directly influence your career's trajectory. Effective scheduling and prioritising tasks ensure that you meet deadlines and maintain high standards of work. Always plan for potential disruptions, allowing some flexibility in your schedule to accommodate unexpected changes or delays. Utilise tools and apps designed for project management to keep track of your tasks and deadlines.

Action Steps:1. Review at least one contract per month with a mentor to build your confidence and understanding

2. Engage in monthly role-playing exercises to sharpen your communication skills, especially in difficult scenarios

3. Implement a time management tool, and each week, spend an hour planning your schedule, ensuring you allocate time for unexpected tasks or delays.

By incorporating these practices into your routine, you'll not only navigate but also thrive in your electrical career. Each step you take builds your reputation as a reliable, skilled, and savvy electrician.

The Leap to Self-Employment

"The best way to predict the future is to create it." - **Peter Drucker**

Planning Your Business

Embarking on the journey of self-employment in the electrical industry is no mere feat—it's an adventure that begins with solid groundwork. Your business plan isn't just a document; it's your roadmap, detailing the route from where you are now to where you envision your business to be. Let's break down this foundation into its essential components: the business plan essentials, setting up a business structure, and financial planning for startups.

Business Plan Essentials

Imagine building a house without a blueprint. That's what venturing into business without a plan would be like. A well-crafted business plan serves multiple purposes: it clarifies your business idea, sets targets, and determines your strategy to achieve them. It also becomes a crucial tool when dealing with banks and investors.

Start with your executive summary. Although it appears first in the plan, you'll write it last. This is a snapshot of your business, a concise outline of what your business is and why it will be successful. Here, you need to hook the reader with clarity and passion but save the deep dive for later sections.

Next, tackle the company description. This is where you detail what your business does and what market needs it addresses. Highlight the advantages your electrical business holds over competitors. Perhaps it's your expertise in sustainable energy solutions or superior customer service; whatever your USP (Unique Selling Proposition), make it shine here.

Market analysis follows, requiring research but paying off by informing your strategy. Who are your potential clients? What geography are you covering? What's the competition like? Understanding the landscape will help you position your business effectively.

The organisation and management section should outline your business's structure. Are you flying solo, or do you have partners? Perhaps you intend to hire contractors. Include bios that highlight the experience and skills that you and your team bring to the table.

Service or product line section should describe what you're

offering. Are you specializing in installations, repairs, or both? What makes your service unique or superior? This section should answer these questions.

Finally, sales strategies, marketing plans, and funding requests. How will you attract and retain customers? How much money do you need to start, and how will you use it? These are critical questions that need detailed answers.

Setting Up a Business Structure

Deciding on the structure of your business is not just a bureaucratic step; it affects your liability, tax obligations, and potential growth. In the UK, you can operate as a sole trader, a partnership, or a limited company. Each has its merits and limitations.

As a sole trader, you get to keep all your profits after tax, but your personal and business assets are considered one and the same, which could be risky. Partnerships are similar but include more than one person sharing the profits and responsibilities.

A limited company offers limited liability, meaning your personal assets are protected in case things go south. It can also be more tax-efficient and enhance your credibility with customers and suppliers. However, it comes with more reporting and management responsibilities.

Each structure has different registration processes with HM

Revenue and Customs (HMRC) and different paperwork requirements. Choosing the right structure is crucial: consider your financial situation, the level of risk you are comfortable with, and your future business goals.

Financial Planning for Startups

Financial planning can seem daunting, but it's just about understanding where your money is going and planning where it should go. Start with estimating your startup costs. Break these down into one-time costs (like equipment and incorporation fees) and ongoing costs (like rent, utilities, salaries, and marketing expenses). This will give you a clear picture of the initial capital you need.

Next, project your cash flow for at least the first year. This involves knowing when you expect to receive money and when your bills are due. Cash flow is the lifeblood of your business; managing it poorly is one of the main reasons new businesses fail.

Don't forget to set aside money for taxes. As an electrician, you'll likely be paying income tax, National Insurance, and possibly VAT, depending on your turnover. Consider getting an accountant who understands the nuances of tax planning and can help you take advantage of any relevant deductions and allowances.

Lastly, consider how you will manage financial risk. This could involve setting aside a contingency fund to cover unexpected expenses or taking out insurance policies relevant to your business activities.

Starting your own electrical business is exciting, and while the challenges can be daunting, the rewards of seeing your own enterprise grow can be immensely satisfying. With a robust business plan, the right legal structure, and sound financial planning, you'll not just survive in the world of self-employment; you'll thrive.

Branding and Marketing

Creating a Brand Identity

When you're diving into the electrifying world of self-employment, your brand is essentially your promise to your customer. It's what they see, think, and feel about your electrical services. Crafting a compelling brand identity isn't just about choosing a catchy name or a flashy logo (though those are certainly part of the equation). It's about building a reputation that speaks of reliability, expertise, and innovation in the electrical field.

First things first, you need to understand who you are as a business. What values drive you? Perhaps it's reliability, speed, or an emphasis on sustainable, energy-efficient solutions. These values are the backbone of your brand identity—they will guide your decisions and help align your brand with your target customers' expectations.

Next, consider your visual identity. This includes your logo, colour scheme, typeface, and overall design aesthetics. These elements should reflect your business values and appeal to your ideal customer. For instance, blue and white are popular colours in the utilities sector, suggesting professionalism and trustworthiness. Your logo should be simple yet memorable, ensuring it can work across various media, from your van's paint job to your business cards.

Remember, consistency is key. Once you've established your visual and core value elements, stick to them across all your platforms and interactions. Consistent branding not only increases your visibility but also builds credibility and trust, which are crucial in gaining and retaining clients.

Marketing Strategies for Electricians

Now that you have your brand identity nailed down, it's time to shout it from the rooftops—or, more accurately, showcase it where your potential clients are most likely to notice. Marketing for electricians doesn't need to be overly complex or expensive. It's about being strategic and resourceful.

Start with the low-hanging fruit: word-of-mouth. In the trades, reputation is everything. Encourage your satisfied customers to refer you to others. Perhaps offer a referral discount or a future service incentive. People are far more likely to trust a recommendation from a friend or family member than any advertisement.

In addition to traditional advertising methods like local newspaper ads or flyers, direct mail campaigns can be particularly effective. Target homes that are old enough to likely need electrical upgrades or repairs. Include a compelling call to action, like a free safety inspection or a discount on their first service call.

Don't overlook the power of community involvement. Participate in local events, sponsor local sports teams, or give a talk at community centres about electrical safety. These activities not only increase your visibility but also establish you as a community-minded, approachable expert.

Online Presence and Social Media

In today's digital age, having an online presence is non-negotiable. It's one of the first places potential customers will go to check out your services, read reviews, and get a feel for your brand. Start with a professional, easy-to-navigate website. Highlight your services, display certifications and licenses, and feature customer testimonials. Make sure your contact information is easy to find and consider adding an online booking system to streamline the process.

Social media is another crucial tool. Platforms like Facebook, Instagram, and LinkedIn can help you reach a broader audience. Share before-and-after photos of your projects, post tips on electrical safety, or explain the benefits of regular maintenance checks. These posts not just showcase your expertise but also keep your audience engaged.

Remember, consistency on social media means regular posting. Tools like Hootsuite or Buffer can help you schedule posts in advance, making this part of your marketing strategy less time-consuming. Engage with your followers by responding to comments and messages. Building relationships with potential customers can transform them into actual customers.

Engaging with online reviews is also vital. Respond professionally to all reviews, addressing any concerns and thanking customers for their feedback. Positive interactions improve your reputation and can turn a negative review into a positive future prospect.

In conclusion, branding and marketing might seem like daunting tasks, especially when you're keen to get out there and start wiring up a storm. But remember, a solid foundation in these areas not only sets you apart from the competition but also sets you up for sustainable success. So, take these tasks seriously, and you'll likely find that your electrical business isn't just surviving, but thriving.

Navigating Legal Requirements

Compliance and Insurance

So, you're ready to take the plunge into self-employment as an electrician. Great decision! But before you can start wiring up your new enterprise, there's some crucial groundwork to be laid in terms of legal requirements. First up, let's talk about compliance and insurance—two staples that will safeguard not just your business, but also your peace of mind.

In the UK, if you're performing electrical work, you must ensure compliance with certain national standards and regulations. For electricians, the most recognised accreditation comes from bodies like the National Inspection Council for Electrical Installation Contracting (NICEIC), or the Electrotechnical Certification Scheme (ECS). These accreditations not only validate your skills and professionalism but also reassure your clients that you adhere to the highest standards of safety and quality.

Insurance is your next big checkpoint. At a minimum, you'll need public liability insurance. This covers you for any injuries or damage to property caused by your work, which, let's face it, is critical given the nature of the job. You might also consider other types of insurance, such as professional indemnity insurance, which protects you against claims of poor workmanship or professional negligence. Remember, being adequately insured not only shields you against unexpected mishaps but also boosts your credibility as a trustworthy professional.

Understanding UK Regulations for Electricians

Moving on to regulations, and yes, it might sound a tad dry, but navigating this maze is essential for keeping your business compliant and out of legal hot water. The UK's regulatory framework for electrical installation work is robust, designed to ensure safety and competency in the industry.

The cornerstone of UK electrical regulations is the BS7671, also known as the Wiring Regulations, which outline the standards for electrical installations. If your work involves designing, building, verifying, or maintaining electrical systems, familiarity with these regulations isn't just recommended—it's essential.

Moreover, if you're planning to work on buildings, be aware of the Part P Building Regulations, which govern electrical safety in homes across England and Wales. These regulations mandate that most fixed domestic electrical installation work complies with all relevant building regulations. Therefore, if your services include installations in bathrooms, kitchens, or outdoors, getting to grips with Part P should be high on your priority list.

Remember, ignorance isn't a defence when it comes to regulatory compliance. Make use of resources like the Health and Safety Executive (HSE) guidelines or local council building control departments—they can offer invaluable guidance and help you navigate the regulatory terrain.

GDPR and Data Handling

Last but definitely not least, let's touch on the General Data Protection Regulation (GDPR) and data handling. In our increasingly digital world, you're going to collect, store, and possibly even share personal data, whether it's client contact details or payment information. Understanding how to handle this data responsibly is not just good practice—it's the law.

GDPR came into effect in May 2018 and it imposes obligations on all businesses, big or small, about how they handle personal data. For you, compliance means ensuring that personal data is gathered legally and under strict conditions, and those who collect and manage it are obliged to protect it from misuse and exploitation, as well as to respect the rights of data owners.

To stay compliant, start by ensuring transparency with your clients about how you collect, use, and store their data. This could mean tweaking your client contracts or terms of service to include clear, concise language about data handling practices. Additionally, consider implementing measures to secure the data you hold—think encrypted storage solutions, robust password policies, and regular security audits.

And don't forget about data minimisation. This principle of GDPR encourages you only to collect data that's necessary for your work. Not only does this reduce the risk of data breaches, but it also builds trust with your clients—they'll appreciate that you're not hoarding their information unnecessarily.

Navigating the legal landscape as a self-employed electrician in the UK can seem daunting at first glance. But with a solid understanding of compliance and insurance, a firm grasp of the regulatory requirements, and a compliant approach to data handling, you'll set a strong foundation for a thriving, resilient electrical business. Remember, these steps aren't just bureaucratic hurdles but crucial protections for you and your business in the highly competitive and regulated world of electrical services.

Recap & Action Items

Congratulations on making it through the pivotal chapter on taking the leap to self-employment as an electrician. You've equipped yourself with the foundational knowledge to plan, brand, and legally structure your budding business. Let's ensure this isn't just another read. It's time to turn these insights into concrete actions that pave your path to success.

Firstly, revisit the essentials of your business plan. Have you clearly defined your business goals, target market, and competitive analysis? Ensure your business plan is not just a document but a roadmap that guides every business decision. If you haven't already, set aside time this week to refine this document, making it as clear and actionable as possible.

Secondly, branding isn't just about a catchy name or a smart logo. It encompasses who you are as a business and how customers perceive you. Reflect on your brand identity. Does it align with the values and services you want to project? If you're unsure, consider seeking feedback from peers or potential customers. Begin sketching out a marketing strategy that uses both traditional methods like local ads and modern tactics like social media to reach your audience effectively. Allocate a few hours each week to boost your online presence, ensuring your business is easily discoverable to the digitally-inclined customer.

Lastly, the legalities. It's crucial not to skimp on this part. Double-check your compliance is in line with UK standards, your insurance coverage is adequate, and that you're compliant with GDPR if you're handling customer data. Missteps here can be costly. Schedule consultations with legal experts if you find any gaps in your understanding or compliance.

Remember, starting your own business is both thrilling and challenging. Each step you take builds the foundation of a resilient, thriving enterprise. Stay committed, stay curious, and most importantly, start now. The journey of a thousand miles begins with a single step – make sure yours is in the right direction.

Growing Your Client Base

"Your most unhappy customers are your greatest source of learning." - Bill Gates

Finding New Clients

Let's dive into the art of attracting new clients. As an electrician ready to spark up your career, understanding how to expand your clientele is crucial. It's not just about being great with wires and circuits; it's also about being savvy in how you connect with potential customers. Here, we'll explore three key areas: networking strategies, leveraging local advertising, and using online platforms tailored for electricians.

Networking Strategies

First things first: networking. It's the age-old art of making and maintaining connections that can drive your business forward.

But, how do you network effectively in a world where everyone seems to be selling something? It's simpler than it sounds, and much more about genuine connections than handing out business cards like they're going out of fashion.

Start by identifying local business events and trade shows related to your industry. These are goldmines for meeting potential clients and other tradespeople who might refer clients to you in the future. Remember, the key here is engagement. Be genuinely interested in what others have to say. Ask questions, offer your insights, and discuss common challenges. It's about creating lasting impressions that could lead to collaborative opportunities or direct business.

Joining local business groups or forums, including those not directly related to the electrical field, can also broaden your horizon. For instance, participating in a local chamber of commerce or a business networking group can expose you to business owners and residential clients who might need your services down the line.

Let's not overlook the power of the digital space for networking. LinkedIn, though often viewed as a corporate platform, is a fantastic tool for tradespeople too. Make a profile that highlights your skills, past projects, and specialisations. Connect with local businesses and participate in discussions. Regular updates and posts about your work can keep you top of mind for your connections.

Leveraging Local Advertising

Next up, let's harness the potential of local advertising. In the digital age, local advertising has taken on new forms, ranging from online ads to traditional flyers. The trick is to find the right mix that works for you and your local area.

Consider the demographics of your target market. Are they likely to read the local newspaper? If so, a well-placed advert could do wonders. Newspapers might feel a bit old-school, but they have a dedicated readership that could be looking for a reliable electrician.

Flyers and local mail drops can also be effective, especially if you offer a discount or a free safety check for new customers. This approach not only spreads the word about your services but also gives potential clients an incentive to contact you.

Don't underestimate the power of online local advertising either. Tools like Google My Business allow you to appear in local search results and on Google Maps, which is perfect when someone nearby searches for an electrician. Encourage satisfied customers to leave reviews on your profile to enhance your visibility and credibility.

Online Platforms for Electricians

Finally, let's talk about tapping into the specialised online platforms designed for tradespeople like you. These platforms can be a gateway to new clients who are actively seeking your specific services.

Websites like Checkatrade and Rated People allow electricians to register and showcase their services. Potential clients often visit these sites to find highly recommended professionals, making them an excellent platform for gaining visibility. The key here is to maintain a robust profile with plenty of customer reviews. Positive feedback is the currency of these platforms and can significantly influence potential clients' decisions.

Additionally, consider the benefits of service-specific platforms such as Nextdoor, where local communities connect to share recommendations and services. Being active on a platform like this can position you as the go-to electrician in your neighbourhood.

Social media platforms shouldn't be overlooked either. Platforms like Facebook and Instagram offer the ability to run targeted ads to reach potential clients in your area. You can showcase your completed projects, share customer testimonials, and even provide quick tips on electrical safety. This not only builds your brand but also establishes your authority in the electrical field.

By exploring these avenues—networking effectively, cleverly

leveraging local advertising, and making the most of online platforms—you can significantly broaden your client base. Each approach has its strengths, and when combined, they can create a comprehensive strategy to help you attract and secure new clients. Keep your approach personal and professional, and you'll find your client list growing in no time.

Customer Relationship Management

Building Client Trust

Trust is the cornerstone of any successful business relationship, especially in a field as integral to daily life as electrical services. When you start out, your client's trust is not given; it is earned. This can be achieved through consistent performance, but there are also proactive steps you can take to accelerate this process.

Firstly, always be transparent with your clients. Whether it's discussing project timelines, costs, or potential roadblocks, clear communication is key. For example, if a project is likely to go over budget due to unforeseen complications, inform your client at the earliest opportunity and explain why. This approach not only prepares them for the unexpected but also shows that you value honesty over making a quick profit.

Additionally, consider your professional appearance and the presentation of your work area. Showing up in a clean, branded uniform and keeping your work area tidy might seem trivial, but they go a long way in establishing a professional image. Remember, every interaction with your client reflects your business's values.

Finally, certifications and continuous professional development can significantly bolster trust. By staying updated with the latest industry standards and technologies, you reassure your clients that they are receiving top-notch, compliant services. This commitment to excellence is what transforms first-time clients into lifelong patrons.

Managing Client Expectations

Setting realistic expectations is vital to maintaining and growing your client base. This starts from the initial consultation and continues throughout your relationship with the client. Always provide clear, detailed written quotes and timelines. This documentation not only serves as a reference point but also minimises the risk of misunderstandings.

However, managing expectations isn't just about aligning on the specifics of a project; it's also about managing day-to-day communications. Be proactive in updating your clients about the progress of their projects. If you anticipate delays or additional costs, inform them immediately. This continuous stream of information helps to manage their expectations and keeps them engaged in the process.

Customer education is another powerful tool in your arsenal.

Educating your clients about the work involved, the materials used, and why certain processes are necessary helps demystify your services. This knowledge makes them more appreciative of the value you provide and sets a realistic frame of reference for what to expect.

Long-term Client Retention Strategies

Retaining clients over the long term requires more than just delivering excellent services; it involves nurturing a relationship that goes beyond transactional interactions. One effective strategy is implementing a follow-up system. After completing a job, send a thank you note or make a follow-up call to ensure that the client is satisfied with the work. This shows that you care about their experience and are open to feedback, which can be invaluable.

Loyalty programs can also be an excellent strategy for long-term retention. Offering discounts on future services or implementing a referral system not only incentivises repeat business but also turns your existing client base into advocates for your brand.

Lastly, keep your clients informed about new services or technologies that might benefit them. For instance, if you start offering smart home installation services, reach out to past clients who might be interested. This not only keeps your business relevant but also shows your clients that you are evolving in your field and keeping their best interests in mind.

By focusing on these three key areas of customer relationship management, you can build a robust foundation for a thriving electrical service business. Remember, at the heart of CRM is the understanding that your relationship with each client is a journey, not merely a series of transactions. Navigate this journey with care, and your business will not only grow but also stand the test of time in a competitive market.

Expanding Services

When you're beginning your journey as an electrician, it's crucial to not only establish a solid foundation of clients but also to continuously look for ways to broaden your service offerings. This not only increases your revenue but also makes your business more resilient against market fluctuations. Let's dive into how you can identify new service opportunities, master the art of upselling and cross-selling, and diversify your business to stay ahead in the competitive electrical industry.

Identifying New Service Opportunities

Staying relevant and competitive in the electrical business means you need to keep a keen eye on emerging trends and technologies. One of the first steps in expanding your services is identifying new opportunities that align with your expertise and customer needs.

Start by conducting market research. See what services are in high demand but low supply within your area. Are homeowners looking for smart home installations? Is there a growing number of electric car owners who might need charging stations? Or perhaps, with the increase in home offices, there's a surge in demand for enhanced electrical systems to support more electronics and higher usage.

Engage with your current clients during service calls. Ask them about their future needs and the problems they face with their existing electrical systems. This direct feedback is invaluable and can guide you towards services that will genuinely benefit your client base.

Additionally, keep an eye on industry standards and regulations. Changes in building codes or energy efficiency requirements can create opportunities for specialised services like energy audits or retrofitting older installations with new, compliant materials.

Upselling and Cross-Selling

Once you've identified potential new services, the next step is to develop your skills in upselling and cross-selling. These strategies are not just about increasing sales; they're about providing added value to your clients, enhancing their satisfaction and loyalty.

Upselling involves encouraging the purchase of a more expensive or upgraded version of what is being bought, while cross-selling invites customers to buy related or complementary items. However, these must be approached with sensitivity and tact; they should feel like genuine recommendations rather than sales pitches.

For instance, if a client plans to renovate their kitchen, you might upsell them from standard lighting fixtures to high-efficiency LED systems that not only last longer but also reduce energy costs. This is an upsell that offers immediate value and is likely to be well-received.

Cross-selling, on the other hand, could be suggesting the installation of smoke detectors or security systems if you're already working on their electrical wiring. Explain the benefits and convenience of addressing these needs concurrently with the current project.

The key to success in upselling and cross-selling is your ability to educate your clients about the benefits and savings of the upgraded or additional services. Always ensure that what you are offering fits their needs and provides real value.

Diversifying Your Business Offerings

Diversification is your safeguard against market fluctuations and client churn. By expanding your range of services, you not only capture and retain a wider client base but also buffer your business against seasonal dips and economic downturns.

Consider branching into related areas such as renewable energy installations like solar panels or wind turbines. As the world moves towards greener solutions, being proficient in these areas can set you apart from competitors and align you with future market trends.

Another approach is to offer maintenance contracts. Regular check-ups and maintenance provide steady work and help build long-term relationships with your clients. They also make your business the first contact in case of any major repairs or upgrades, thus providing additional revenue streams.

Training and certification in newer technologies and regulations not only broaden your service offerings but also enhance your reputation as a qualified and up-to-date electrician. This can be particularly appealing to corporate clients and industries that must comply with strict standards and regulations.

Lastly, consider strategic partnerships with other tradespeople who offer complementary services, such as plumbers or HVAC technicians. These partnerships allow you to offer package deals or referrals, thereby expanding your network and providing your clients with a full spectrum of home improvement services.

In conclusion, expanding your services as an electrician involves a mix of market awareness, client engagement, strategic selling, and continuous learning. By staying adaptive and proactive, you can not only meet the changing needs of your clients but also ensure that your electrical business thrives and grows in an ever-evolving industry.

Recap & Action Items

Congratulations on completing this crucial chapter on Growing Your Client Base! You're now armed with effective strategies to find new clients, manage your relationships with them, and expand your services to ensure your electrical business isn't just surviving, but thriving.

Let's distill what you've learnt into concrete steps you can take right away to put these ideas into action.

1. **Networking Strategies**: Start by marking your calendar for at least two networking events this month, whether they're local trade shows, business meetups, or seminars relevant to the electrical industry. Remember, the goal is to connect, not just collect business cards. Focus on building genuine relationships.

2. **Leveraging Local Advertising:** Design a simple, compelling flyer highlighting your services and special offers. Distribute these in your local community centres, libraries, and also consider a small ad in your local newspaper. Keep the message clear and direct, focusing on how you can solve common electrical issues quickly and efficiently.

3. **Online Platforms for Electricians**: Register on at least three online platforms dedicated to home services or local businesses. Fill out your profiles completely, ensuring that you include client testimonials and photos of completed jobs to

build credibility.

4. **Building Client Trust**: Always communicate clearly and honestly with your clients. Let them know what you can do, how much it will cost, and how long it will likely take. No surprises means a happier client.

5. **Managing Client Expectations**: Set realistic timelines and always keep clients updated on progress. If delays occur, communicate these as soon as possible, along with your plan to get back on track.

6. **Long-term Client Retention Strategies**: Implement a follow-up system. Send out a thank you note after a job completion, and perhaps a reminder when it's time for an electrical safety check. Consider offering a discount for their next service when they refer a new client.

7. **Identifying New Service Opportunities**: Keep abreast of the latest trends in the electrical industry. Are there new technologies or regulations? Offering to upgrade old systems or install new technology can be a great way to add value for your clients.

8. **Upselling and Cross-Selling**: On your next job, try recommending a service that complements what the client has already asked for. For example, if you're updating electrical panels, suggest checking and upgrading indoor and outdoor lighting if necessary.

9.**Diversifying Your Business Offerings**: Think about what other services you can provide that will make your business a one-stop solution. Could you offer energy efficiency audits, or perhaps branch into smart home installations?

By taking these steps, you're not just working in your business; you're working on your business. Each action is a stepping stone towards building a robust, dynamic, and successful electrical service company. Dive in, the opportunities are waiting!

Financial Fluency for Electricians

"We buy things we don't need with money we don't have to impress people we don't like." - Dave Ramsey

Managing Finances

Navigating the financial waters of your new career as an electrician doesn't have to feel like you're sailing through a storm. With the right tools and know-how, you can keep your books as tidy as your toolbox and ensure your cash flow keeps flowing smoothly. Let's dive into the essentials of managing your finances, covering everything from bookkeeping basics to invoicing and payments.

Bookkeeping Basics

Think of bookkeeping as the map that shows where your money is coming from and where it's going. It's crucial, not just for keeping the taxman happy, but for giving you a clear picture of your financial health. Get this right, and you're already off to a great start.

First off, you need to choose your method. Single-entry bookkeeping is straightforward and involves recording each transaction once, either as income or expense. It's simple and might be all you need when you're just starting. However, as your business grows, you might want to consider double-entry bookkeeping. This method involves recording each transaction twice, once as a debit and once as a credit. It sounds more complicated, but it gives you a fuller picture of your financial situation.

Investing in good accounting software can be a game-changer, especially ones that cater to the needs of tradespeople. Look for features that allow you to track your expenses, send invoices, and even prepare financial reports. Many programs also link directly to your bank account, automating some of the more tedious aspects of the job.

Remember, consistency is key. Set aside regular time each week to update your books. This might seem like a chore now, but it will save you a mountain of stress come tax season.

As your business grows and your bookkeeping becomes more complex, you might consider outsourcing this task to a professional. Hiring a bookkeeper or accountant can free up your time, ensure accuracy, and provide expert insights into your financial health. This can be especially beneficial if you're not confident in managing the books yourself or if you want to focus more on growing your business rather than getting bogged down in financial details.

Managing Cash Flow

Cash flow is the lifeblood of your business. It's all about timing—ensuring that your incoming cash (from jobs completed, invoices paid, etc.) aligns with your outgoings (like supplier costs, equipment purchases, and personal withdrawals).

To manage your cash flow effectively, start by setting up a separate business bank account. This makes tracking your business finances easier and more transparent.

Next, get a grip on your expenses. It's easy for costs to spiral, especially in the early days when you're eager to take on new jobs and might be investing in a lot of new equipment. Keep a close eye on what's going out each month, and don't forget to factor in irregular expenses like insurance or taxes.

Invoice promptly and follow up on payments. The sooner you invoice after a job, the sooner you get paid. Make your payment terms clear from the get-go (30 days is standard, but you might choose to shorten this) and don't be shy about sending a polite reminder if a payment is late.

Finally, consider setting up an emergency fund. This isn't just sound personal finance advice; it's a solid business strategy. Having a buffer can help you manage the ups and downs of self-employment without panicking or falling into debt.

Invoicing and Payments

Invoicing might not be the most exciting part of your job, but it's absolutely critical. Your invoices are the requests for payment that you send to clients after completing a job. They should be clear, professional, and include all the necessary details to ensure you get paid the right amount, on time.

Each invoice should include:- Your name, address, and contact information

- The client's name and address

- A unique invoice number

- The date of the invoice

- A clear description of what the charges are for

- The total amount due

- Your payment terms (e.g., due within30 days).- Your payment details (e.g., bank account number).

Software can really help streamline this process. Many accounting programs offer customizable invoice templates that not only look professional but also automatically include all the necessary details. They can also send reminders to clients about upcoming or overdue payments, which takes some of the awkwardness out of chasing up late payers.

Offering multiple payment options can also accelerate the process. Besides traditional methods like bank transfers or cheques, consider accepting payments through online platforms. Many customers appreciate the convenience of paying via PayPal or similar services, which can mean quicker payments for you.

By getting your invoicing right, you're more likely to see a steady stream of income, which is crucial for maintaining good cash flow and ultimately, a healthy business.

Remember, managing finances effectively is a foundational skill that will support every aspect of your career as an electrician. With these practices in place, you're not just working hard with your tools, but you're also working smart with your resources.

Taxation Essentials

Understanding UK Tax Obligations

Navigating the maze of tax obligations is crucial, not just to keep the taxman at bay, but to ensure you're not accidentally giving away a slice of your hard-earned cash that could legally stay in your pocket. As a newly qualified electrician, understanding your tax obligations is the bedrock of your financial structure.

Firstly, if you're self-employed, you need to register with HMRC. This is how you tell them you're now playing in the big leagues of tax-paying workers. Once registered, you'll pay Income Tax through Self Assessment. This means every year, you'll need to fill out a form that details your earnings and expenses. The deadline for online submissions is January 31st for the tax year that ended the previous April. Miss this deadline, and you'll face a penalty, starting at £100 and increasing over time, so punctuality is key.

National Insurance Contributions (NICs) are another critical piece of the puzzle. These contribute towards your state benefits, like the State Pension and Jobseeker's Allowance. You'll pay two types of NICs: Class 2 if your profits are £6,725 or more a year, and Class 4 if your profits exceed £12,570. These rates and thresholds can change, so keep an eye on the HMRC website for the latest figures.

Understanding these obligations is your first step towards savvy financial management. Make sure you keep accurate records of all your income and expenses. It's not just good practice; it's your financial defence against overpaying tax.

VAT for Electricians

VAT, or Value Added Tax, is a bit like a relay race where each participant adds a bit of value before passing it on. As an electrician, you'll need to understand when to register for VAT, how to charge it, and how to handle it correctly.

You must register for VAT if your turnover of VAT taxable goods and services supplied within the UK for the previous 12 months is more than the current VAT threshold of £90,000. You can also register voluntarily if it suits your business model, even if you're under the threshold. This might sound counterintuitive, but doing so can actually enhance your credibility and professionalism, showing potential business clients that you're a serious player.

Once registered, you'll charge VAT at 20% on most of the services you provide, unless they're exempt or subject to a reduced rate. This amount then needs to be reported and paid to HMRC through your VAT returns, usually every quarter.

Keeping meticulous records here is non-negotiable. You'll need to track all your VAT expenses because these can often be reclaimed. For instance, if you buy a new piece of equipment for your business, the VAT you paid can potentially be reclaimed, lowering your overall costs.

Understanding VAT is not just about compliance; it's about making the system work for you. So, dive into the details, keep flawless records, and ensure you're reclaiming wherever possible.

Maximising Tax Deductions

Every penny counts when you're running your own electrical business, and tax deductions are the bread and butter of keeping more of your money in your pocket. Understanding what you can deduct from your taxes is like finding money in old jeans —

a small victory dance is entirely appropriate.

First off, let's talk about expenses. Almost any cost that is solely and directly related to your business can be deducted. This includes the obvious things like tools, uniforms, and vehicle costs if you use it for work. But don't forget about the less obvious items. Do you use your home as an office? Portions of your heating, electricity, Internet, and even rent can sometimes be deducted.

Travel expenses can get a bit tricky. You can claim the costs of travel to and from jobs, but commuting from your home to a fixed office typically can't be claimed. Keep those receipts and log those miles — they add up. Meals during long jobs away from home can also be deductible, but remember that the rules can be stringent, and it's essential to ensure they are wholly, exclusively and necessarily in the performance of your business duties.

Training courses are another often-overlooked area. As a newly qualified electrician, if you take additional courses to improve your skills specifically for your business, these costs can generally be deducted. It's an investment in your business and reduces your taxable income — a win-win.

Lastly, don't overlook the Annual Investment Allowance (AIA). This allows you to deduct the full value of an item that qualifies for the allowance from your profits before tax. This could be anything from new drills to a brand-new van, as long as it's used for business.

By maximizing your tax deductions, you ensure that you're not paying more tax than necessary. It's about knowing the rules and applying them effectively. Remember, every allowable deduction you claim could reduce your tax bill, freeing up funds that can be reinvested back into growing your business or lining your pockets.

Understanding and managing these elements of taxation will not only help you comply with UK laws but will empower you to take control of your financial health. Keep your records straight, stay informed on changes, and use every tool at your disposal to ensure your business thrives through savvy financial management.

Profit Maximisation

When you're starting out as an electrician, every penny counts. It's not just about earning more, but also about keeping more of what you earn by employing smart strategies to maximise your profits. Let's dive into some ways you can tighten the bolts on your financial operations to see your margins improve.

Cost Control Strategies

The first step to fattening your wallet is to trim the fat from your expenses. Cost control is the art of reducing expenses without cutting corners on quality, which could harm your reputation and drive customers away. Here are several tactics you can use to keep your expenses in check:

1. **Buy Smart**: As an electrician, your tools and materials can be a significant expense. Always look for ways to buy better. Consider bulk purchases for items you use frequently, such as cables, switches, and fittings, to benefit from lower prices. Also, establish good relationships with suppliers – they might offer you discounts as a regular customer or let you know when they have a sale coming up.

2. **Go Energy Efficient**: Whether it's the vehicle you drive between jobs or the equipment you use, opting for energy-efficient options can save you a bundle in the long run. More fuel-efficient vehicles, LED lighting in your workspace, and energy-saving tools can reduce your monthly bills considerably.

3. **Regular Maintenance**: Keeping your tools and machinery in top condition prevents costly repairs and replacements. Schedule regular check-ups and maintain your equipment well. It's like keeping the health of your business in peak condition – prevention is always cheaper than a cure.

4. **Outsource Wisely**: Sometimes, outsourcing certain tasks can be more cost-effective than doing them yourself. For example, if bookkeeping isn't your forte, hiring a professional might not only free up your time to focus on electrical work but also ensure you're not bleeding money due to financial errors.

5. **Review Expenses Regularly**: Make it a habit to review your expenses regularly. Look for patterns and identify areas

where you can cut back without affecting your service quality. Sometimes, small tweaks in how you operate can lead to significant savings.

Profit Margin Improvement

Increasing your profit margin isn't just about cutting costs; it's also about enhancing the value of what you offer. Here are some tips to help you charge more without losing customers:

1. **Specialise**: Consider specialising in a niche area of electrical work that commands higher fees. Whether it's smart home installations, solar panels, or high-end commercial projects, specialising can set you apart from the competition and allow you to charge more for your expertise.

2. **Improve Your Skills**: Continuous learning and certification can make you more competent and confident. The more skilled you are, the quicker and more efficiently you can complete jobs, which increases your hourly or project-based earnings.

3. **Offer Great Service**: Sometimes, it's the little things that count. Being friendly, punctual, and tidy might seem trivial, but they enhance customer satisfaction and can lead to repeat business and referrals, which cost nothing but can significantly boost your income.

4. **Bundle Services**: When you offer bundled services, customers perceive they are getting better value, which can make them

more inclined to choose you over a competitor. For example, offering an inspection package along with repair services can increase your earnings from a single visit.

5. **Use High-Quality Materials**: This might sound counterintuitive when talking about cost-cutting, but using high-quality materials can reduce the frequency of failures and callbacks. This improves customer satisfaction and the likelihood of positive reviews and referrals, which can lead to more business at better rates.

Financial Health Indicators

To ensure the long-term success of your electrical business, you need to keep your finger on the pulse of its financial health. Here are some key indicators to monitor:

1. **Cash Flow**: This is the lifeblood of your business. Ensure you have more cash coming in than going out. Tools like cash flow forecasts can help you anticipate and plan for future financial needs.

2. **Gross Profit Margin**: Regularly calculate your gross profit margin (total sales minus the cost of goods sold). A declining margin could be a red flag that your costs are rising or you're underpricing your services.

3. **Debtor Days**: Keep track of how quickly customers are paying you. A high number of debtor days means your cash is tied up

in unpaid invoices, affecting your liquidity.

4. **Return on Investment (ROI)**: Measure the return on investment for significant expenses like new equipment or marketing campaigns. This helps you understand whether those investments are paying off.

5. **Break-even Point**: Know your break-even point – the amount you need to earn each month to cover all your expenses. This knowledge helps you set financial goals and assess the viability of business decisions.

By mastering these areas – controlling costs, improving margins, and monitoring financial health indicators – you can set your electrical business on a path to not just survive, but thrive. Remember, financial fluency isn't just about keeping books; it's about making strategic decisions that bolster your bottom line.

Recap & Action Items

Congratulations on powering through the essentials of financial fluency! You've now got the tools to manage your finances, understand your taxation, and maximise your profits. Let's make sure you transform this knowledge into action to electrify your career prospects and financial health.

First off, tackle the basics of bookkeeping. Set aside time each week to update your records. This isn't just about compliance; it's about creating a dashboard for your business's financial health. Consider using software that caters to small businesses; this can automate much of the heavy lifting and reduce errors. Remember, good habits formed early can save you a world of stress down the line.

Next, streamline your cash flow. Start by reviewing the payment terms you offer clients and the speed with which you issue invoices. Could these be tightened up? Faster invoicing often leads to faster payments. Also, keep a keen eye on your expenditures. It's easy for costs to creep up unnoticed.

On the taxation front, ensure you're crystal clear on your obligations. The HM Revenue & Customs website is a treasure trove of resources, and it's wise to check in regularly for updates, especially about VAT if your turnover is near the threshold. Consider seeking advice from a tax professional—it can be a worthwhile investment to safeguard against overpayment or penalties.

For maximising tax deductions, maintain a meticulous log of all business-related expenses. From vehicle costs to workwear, make sure you're claiming everything you're entitled to. Often, it's the small things that add up to significant savings.

Lastly, let's talk profit maximisation. Regularly review your service pricing. Are you charging what you're worth? Adjust as necessary, especially as you gain more experience and expertise. Keep an eye on your financial health indicators like net profit margin and return on investment. These aren't just numbers; they're reflections of your business strategy in action.

Start today by choosing one action from each of these areas to implement this week. Success in business, as in electricity, requires both a sound understanding of theory and the practical ability to apply that knowledge effectively. Charge up your career by keeping these circuits of financial management in excellent working order.

Technology in Electrical Work

"It is only through innovation and technology that we advance beyond the limitations of today." - Elon Musk

Modern Tools and Technologies

As a newly qualified electrician, you're embarking on an exciting journey in an industry that is constantly evolving. The key to staying competitive and delivering high-quality work lies in embracing the modern tools and technologies that are revolutionizing the trade. This chapter aims to equip you with the knowledge and tools necessary to not only meet but exceed the expectations of modern electrical work standards.

Advancements in Electrical Tools

In the ever-evolving world of electrical work, staying ahead means keeping up with the latest gadgets and gizmos that make your job not just easier, but more efficient and safe. As a newly minted electrician, you're stepping into an era where the tools you carry are just as smart as they are essential.

Take, for instance, the digital multimeter with Bluetooth connectivity. Imagine performing diagnostics on a complex system from your smartphone or tablet, without having to hover over live circuits. These devices not only increase safety but also store data for future reference, allowing you to track changes and patterns over time.

Then there's the laser distance measurer, a godsend for any electrician who needs to quickly and accurately scope out large spaces. Gone are the days of fumbling with tape measures in cramped corners. With a laser measurer, you can get precise readings in a fraction of the time, allowing you to move on to the actual work faster.

Another game changer is the thermal imaging camera. Previously a tool for the few due to its hefty price tag, recent models have become more affordable. This technology allows you to see beyond the visible, identifying hot spots and potential hazards before they lead to problems. It's like having X-ray vision, revealing issues hidden behind walls or in electrical cabinets.

Smart Home Technology

Smart home technology is not just a passing trend—it's rapidly becoming a staple in homes across the country, and it's reshaping the electrical industry. As a newcomer, understanding how to integrate, maintain, and troubleshoot these systems can set you apart from more seasoned electricians.

Starting with the basics, smart lighting systems are perhaps the most common entry point. These systems offer more than just convenience; they provide efficiency, with the ability to control lighting remotely, set schedules, and even adjust colour temperatures to suit different times of the day. Mastery of smart lighting systems doesn't just make a home more enjoyable; it can also significantly reduce energy consumption, a selling point you can highlight to prospective clients.

Next up are smart thermostats, which like lighting, offer both comfort and cost savings. These devices learn the habits of the household and adjust heating and cooling accordingly, minimising energy waste. They can be monitored and adjusted from anywhere, providing constant comfort and peace of mind for homeowners.

But smart homes go beyond just lighting and temperature. Integrated security systems, smart locks, and even smart appliances are becoming the norm. These devices require not only electrical know-how but also a bit of IT savvy, as they often involve network configurations and troubleshooting connectivity issues.

Renewable Energy Technologies

As the world shifts towards sustainability, renewable energy technologies are becoming increasingly important. For electricians, this means a whole new landscape of opportunities—and challenges.

Solar power installations are at the forefront. Understanding how to install solar panels, inverters, and storage systems is crucial. These systems are not just about placing panels on a roof; they involve complex electrical systems that must safely integrate with the home's existing electrical grid. The ability to offer solar solutions can significantly expand your service offerings and business prospects.

Wind energy is another area with growing interest, particularly in rural or remote areas. While you might not be installing massive turbines like those seen in wind farms, smaller, residential-scale turbines are becoming more popular as a supplementary power source.

Finally, there's the burgeoning field of electric vehicle (EV) charging stations. With the rise in EV ownership, the demand for home and commercial charging stations is skyrocketing. Installing and maintaining these systems requires understanding not only of the electrical components but also of the specific requirements for different EV models.

Each of these technologies not only helps in reducing carbon footprints but also opens up new revenue streams for you as an electrician. As governments continue to incentivize green technology, being proficient in these areas could not only set you apart but also future-proof your career.

Embracing these modern tools and technologies is not just about keeping up with the trends. It's about setting yourself up for a thriving career in an industry that's as dynamic as it is critical. Whether it's the latest in tool tech, smart home devices, or renewable energy systems, each step forward you take is a step towards a more successful and sustainable practice in the electrical field. As you equip yourself with these advanced tools and knowledge, remember that each skill you acquire not only enhances your capability but also adds a layer of value to the services you offer, making you the electrician of choice for clients who are equally keen on moving towards a smarter, more efficient world.

Software for Electricians

In the ever-evolving world of electrical work, staying ahead isn't just about the wires and switches, but also about mastering the software that can streamline your projects, enhance your customer relations, and keep your finances in check. As a newly qualified electrician, embracing these digital tools can transform the way you work, making you more efficient, connected, and financially savvy.

Project Management Tools

First up, let's talk about project management tools. Think of these as your digital toolbox, essential for keeping your projects, well, on project. These tools are designed to help you plan, execute, and monitor your electrical projects from start to finish. They can be a game changer, especially when you're juggling multiple jobs.

One popular choice is Trello. It's simple to use and visually intuitive, making it easy for you to track each phase of your project. You can set up boards for different projects, create lists for tasks like 'To Do', 'Doing', and 'Done', and move cards as you progress. It's a great way to keep everything transparent and accessible, not just for you but also for any team members or subcontractors you might be working with.

Then there's Asana, which is a bit more robust. It allows you to assign tasks, set deadlines, and even integrate with other tools like Slack for communication, or Google Drive for document storage. Asana can send you reminders before deadlines, helping ensure you never miss a beat.

Using these tools effectively means less time spent on back-and-forth communication and more time getting down to the real work. They can help you visualise your workflow, identify any bottlenecks, and adjust on the fly. This isn't just about staying organised; it's about being dynamic and responsive in your work approach.

Customer Relationship Management Software

Moving on to customer relationship management, or CRM software. This isn't just for the big corporates. As an electrician, your relationship with your clients is your bread and butter. CRM software can help you manage that relationship by keeping track of all interactions, from initial contact to post-job follow-up.

A tool like HubSpot can be incredibly useful here. It allows you to store contact details, communication history, and even project notes all in one place. You can see at a glance when you last spoke to a customer or sent an invoice. It's also handy for setting up reminders for follow-ups or scheduling regular maintenance checks.

For those looking to get a bit more advanced, Salesforce offers a more comprehensive suite of tools that can be customised to your business needs. It can integrate with your project management tools and even your financial software, giving you a complete overview of your customer's journey.

Imagine finishing a job and using your CRM to not only send out an invoice but also to schedule a follow-up visit or ask for a review. This kind of proactive service can really set you apart from the competition and keep your clients coming back.

Financial Management Software

Lastly, let's dive into financial management software. Keeping a tight rein on your finances is crucial, and the right tools can make this much less daunting. Software like QuickBooks or Xero is tailored for small businesses and contractors. They can handle everything from invoicing and payroll to tax returns and expense tracking.

QuickBooks, for instance, offers features like automatic mileage tracking, receipt capture via smartphone, and cash flow insights. It can sync with your bank account and categorise your expenses, making it easier to see where your money is going and to prepare for tax time.

Xero, on the other hand, shines with its real-time financial reporting and easy integration with over 800 third-party apps. This means you can tailor it to work seamlessly with other tools you're using. Also, its dashboard provides a clear view of your financial health at a glance, which can be incredibly empowering when you're trying to make informed business decisions.

Both these tools offer mobile apps, which means you can manage your finances on the go. Whether you're between job sites or checking in from the road, you have all your financial information right at your fingertips. This not only saves time but also reduces the risk of errors that can occur when rushing to catch up on paperwork at the end of a busy day.

By integrating these types of software into your workflow, you not only streamline your operations but also free up more time to focus on what you do best – electrical work. The initial setup might take some time and adjustment, but the long-term benefits of increased efficiency, improved customer relationships, and better financial management can significantly propel your career forward.

Embracing these digital tools is no longer optional; it's essential. They not only help you manage your day-to-day tasks but also support your growth as a business owner and a service provider. As you continue to navigate, innovate, and thrive in your electrical career, these tools will be invaluable companions on your journey.

Staying Updated

In the fast-evolving world of electrical work, staying on the cutting edge isn't just a nice-to-have, it's a necessity. Technologies evolve, standards change, and new innovations appear quicker than a flick of a switch. Let's dive into how you can keep your skills sharp and your knowledge up to date.

Continuing Professional Development

Think of your career as a complex circuit board. Just as a circuit needs a constant power supply to function, your career needs continuous learning to thrive. Continuing Professional Development, or CPD, is the ongoing process of developing, maintaining, and documenting your professional skills.

You might wonder how CPD applies to you, especially after spending years in training to become a qualified electrician. The truth is, learning never stops. The electrical industry is subject to frequent updates in regulations and technology. Engaging in CPD is not only beneficial but often required to ensure compliance and to maintain the validity of your qualifications.

One effective way to engage in CPD is by subscribing to relevant journals and magazines. Publications like 'Electrical Times' and 'Professional Electrician & Installer' provide a wealth of information on the latest industry trends and technologies. They often feature articles written by industry experts on topics ranging from energy-efficient technologies to the latest wiring regulations.

Online platforms offer another avenue for CPD. Websites like the Electrical Contractors' Association (ECA) and the Institution of Engineering and Technology (IET) host a range of online courses, webinars, and interactive content specifically designed for continuing education in the electrical field. These resources allow you to learn at your own pace and, importantly, in your own time.

Remember, the goal of CPD is not just to accumulate knowledge but to apply this knowledge in practical, real-world settings. This not only enhances your skill set but also boosts your career advancement opportunities by keeping you informed and ahead of the curve.

Training and Certifications

As a newly qualified electrician, you have a basic toolkit of skills. However, specialising can make you more valuable and open up new career paths. This is where additional training and certifications come into play. They are your opportunity to deepen your expertise in specific areas such as solar energy installation or smart home technology.

Certifications can particularly boost your credentials. For instance, becoming a Certified Electrical Safety Compliance Professional (CESCP) demonstrates your commitment to electrical safety and can be a significant advantage in industrial or commercial environments. Meanwhile, accreditation in renewable energy installations can position you perfectly in a sector that's set to grow exponentially as the world shifts towards sustainable energy solutions.

Training courses, whether online or in-person, provide hands-on experience and testing on current best practices. Manufacturers of electrical products also often offer training sessions to ensure that electricians are proficient in installing and maintaining their latest products. These can be incredibly valuable as they not only provide certification but also give you direct insight into the practical aspects of new technologies.

Industry Seminars and Workshops

Attending seminars and workshops is not only about learning; it's also an opportunity to network with peers, discuss industry challenges, and share solutions. These events bring together thought leaders, innovators, and experienced professionals from the electrical industry.

Workshops typically focus on practical skills and are often more interactive than seminars. They can range from learning advanced diagnostic techniques to hands-on practice with new types of electrical equipment. Seminars, on the other hand, tend to be more theory-based and are great for delving deeper into topics like electrical safety regulations or the latest research in electrical engineering.

Both seminars and workshops can provide you with insights into emerging trends and regulatory changes that could affect how you work. They also offer a platform to ask questions directly to experts you might not usually have access to. Furthermore, these events can be a great way to discover new tools and technologies firsthand.

Make a habit of checking for upcoming events hosted by industry bodies such as the ECA or local trade associations. Additionally, consider attending broader conferences on construction and technology; these can offer new perspectives and inspire innovative approaches to your work.

In conclusion, staying updated in the ever-changing landscape of electrical work is crucial. It enhances not only your career prospects but also your ability to perform your job safely and effectively. Engage actively in CPD, seek out additional training and certifications, and participate in seminars and workshops. By doing so, you're not just keeping pace; you're setting the pace, ensuring that your career as an electrician is as dynamic and current as the field you've chosen to excel in.

Recap & Action Items

You've just equipped yourself with a comprehensive guide on how today's technology can enhance your career as an electrician. With the latest advancements in electrical tools, you're set to work smarter, not harder. Embracing smart home technology and renewable energy solutions not only positions you as a forward-thinker but also opens up new avenues for business growth and customer satisfaction.

Now, let's translate this newfound knowledge into action. First, assess the tools you currently use daily. Which could be upgraded to a smarter, more efficient version? Perhaps investing in a thermal imaging camera or an advanced multimeter could save you time and increase accuracy in your diagnostics.

Next, consider how software can streamline your operations. Have you adopted a robust project management tool yet? Tools like these can revolutionise how you plan, execute, and review your projects. It might also be time to look into customer relationship management software to keep your client interactions as sharp as your technical skills. Remember, happy clients are returning clients.

Financial management software is another key player; it's crucial for keeping your business's heart beating - its finances. If you haven't already, start exploring options that integrate with the other software you're using. A unified system reduces errors and frees up more of your time to focus on what you do best.

Lastly, never underestimate the importance of continual learning. The landscape of electrical work is ever-evolving, and staying updated through professional development, training, and industry events is essential. Each certificate you earn not only adds to your credibility but also to your ability to handle diverse and complex projects.

Set a goal to attend at least one industry seminar or workshop every quarter. Keep an eye out for advanced certifications in areas like smart home tech and renewable energies, and slot in time each week to read up on the latest in electrical innovations.

By following these steps, you'll not only keep pace with the industry but set yourself apart as a leader in the field. Here's to powering up your career with the right tools, tech, and tenacity!

Ensuring Customer Satisfaction

"The goal as a company is to have customer service that is not just the best but legendary." - Sam Walton

Quality Workmanship

Navigating through the early years of your electrical career, the quality of your workmanship is not just a reflection of your skills but a foundational pillar for building a robust, customer-oriented business. Let's break down what it really takes to ensure your electrical work not only meets but exceeds expectations.

Standards and Compliance

First things first, adhering to standards and compliance isn't just about ticking boxes. It's about understanding the why behind each regulation and how they contribute to safety and efficiency. In the UK, familiarising yourself with the BS7671, also known as the Wiring Regulations, is crucial. These are not just guidelines but standards set out to ensure the safety of electrical installations.

Every job you undertake needs to be compliant with these regulations. But how do you make sure you're on top of it all? Keep your knowledge current by attending workshops, seminars, and refresher courses. Regulations update often, and staying informed is your first line of defence against unintentional non-compliance.

Besides the mandatory regulations, you should also be aware of the Codes of Practice that apply to specific areas like fire alarm systems, emergency lighting, and energy efficiency. These codes provide additional guidance that can elevate the standard of your work from passable to exceptional.

Remember, compliance is not just for avoiding legal pitfalls; it's about ensuring that every electrical system you install or service is optimally safe and functional. This not only protects your customers but boosts your reputation as a diligent and trustworthy electrician.

Quality Control in Electrical Work

Moving on from the nitty-gritty of standards and compliance, let's talk about enforcing quality control on a day-to-day basis. Quality control is like the secret sauce that can set you apart from your competitors. It starts with the basics: using high-quality materials and the right tools. Opt for reputable suppliers and manufacturers whose products comply with UK standards and have proven reliability. Poor quality materials can lead to failures and safety issues down the line, which is a direct hit to your reputation.

Next, focus on your work processes. Are they as efficient and effective as they can be? It's worthwhile to periodically review your methods and workflow. Could you introduce better technology or tools? Is there a way to enhance safety while speeding up the process without compromising the quality of work? For instance, using thermal imaging cameras to check for overheating issues during an inspection could both impress and reassure your clients.

Documentation is another key aspect of quality control. Maintain detailed records of your projects, including what was done, materials used, compliance checks, and testing results. This not only helps in maintaining transparency with your clients but also comes in handy if any discrepancies or issues arise later.

Handling Revisions and Corrections

No matter how skilled you are, there will be times when things don't go as planned. Handling revisions and corrections with grace and professionalism is crucial. When a client points out an issue, your response should be swift and constructive. Assess the situation thoroughly—sometimes what seems like a fault might be a misunderstanding of expectations or miscommunication.

When corrections are needed, communicate openly with your clients about what went wrong and how you plan to fix it. This openness builds trust and reliability. Always follow through on your promises to rectify issues, and ensure the corrected work adheres to all standards and quality expectations.

Moreover, use these instances as learning opportunities. Each revision or correction is a chance to refine your skills and processes. Maybe there's a need to improve your initial assessment procedures or enhance how you communicate project specifics to clients. Reflecting on these situations will help you develop a more robust approach to your work, reducing future errors and increasing customer satisfaction.

In the realm of electrical work, your reputation as a quality service provider is one of your most valuable assets. By focusing on rigorous standards and compliance, implementing robust quality control measures, and handling revisions with professionalism, you solidify your standing as a top-tier electrician. Not only will this dedication to quality craftsmanship lead to satisfied customers, but it will also pave the way for a thriving, successful career in the electrical field. Remember, every wire you twist, every circuit you complete, every client you impress—it all adds up to a portfolio of work that speaks volumes about your commitment to excellence.

Handling Feedback

In the electrician's world, feedback isn't just about glowing reviews or pat-on-the-back moments from satisfied clients. It's a pivotal element that can shape your career, refine your skills, and boost your professional reputation. Let's break down how to handle feedback, respond to complaints, and turn every comment into a stepping stone for growth.

Encouraging Customer Feedback

First off, let's talk about encouraging feedback. In your early days on the job, it might feel a bit daunting to actively seek out what customers think of your work. But here's the thing: feedback is gold. It's your direct line to understanding how your services are perceived and what impact you're making.

Start by creating easy channels for your customers to leave feedback. This could be a simple follow-up email with a link to a feedback form, or even a quick SMS after completing a job. Make sure the process is hassle-free—no one enjoys a cumbersome survey. Keep it short and sweet. Ask specific questions that relate to the quality of your work and their overall satisfaction.

Now, it's not just about collecting feedback; it's also about encouraging honest opinions. Be upfront with your clients. Let them know that their feedback is crucial for your growth as an electrician. Explain that you're eager to learn and improve.

Most customers appreciate a tradesperson who is committed to their craft and will be more inclined to provide constructive criticism if they know it's genuinely welcomed.

Responding to Complaints

No one likes receiving complaints, but they come with the territory. How you handle these can either make or break your reputation. The key? Respond promptly and with poise. When a customer expresses dissatisfaction, take a deep breath and approach the situation with a mindset to resolve it amicably.

Firstly, listen. Really listen. Let the customer fully explain what they're unhappy about without interrupting. Acknowledging their concerns shows that you take their feedback seriously and that you care about providing a solution.

Once you've understood the complaint, apologize sincerely. Even if you believe it wasn't your fault, an apology doesn't mean you're admitting guilt; rather, you're empathizing with their experience under your service. From there, discuss potential solutions. Can the issue be rectified? If so, offer to fix it at a time that suits them. If it's beyond repair, discuss other ways to make amends, perhaps through a discount or refund. This demonstrates goodwill and a commitment to customer satisfaction.

Always follow up after resolving a complaint. A simple message asking if they're satisfied with the solution goes a long way in mending and maintaining a professional relationship. Remember, a well-handled complaint can often lead to a loyal customer who trusts you to right a wrong.

Learning from Feedback

Finally, learning from feedback is what will truly distinguish you as a professional who's committed to excellence. Every piece of feedback is a nugget of insight into how you can enhance your service. Gather your feedback regularly and review it. Look for patterns or recurring comments—these are your indicators of what's working well and what might need a tweak.

Set aside time to reflect on this feedback. For instance, if several clients mention that your work area is left untidy, consider incorporating a cleanup routine post-job. Small changes can have a big impact on customer satisfaction.

Moreover, don't shy away from discussing this feedback with mentors or more experienced colleagues. They can offer a fresh perspective and advice on how to implement changes effectively.

Embrace feedback as a tool for continuous improvement. It's a vital component that fuels your professional development and helps you stand out in a competitive field. By actively seeking out, responding to, and learning from feedback, you're not just doing a job; you're crafting a remarkable career in the electrical field, one satisfied customer at a time.

Aftercare Services

Once the installation is complete and the handshakes are exchanged, the real game begins. Aftercare services aren't just add-ons; they are crucial pillars that support your reputation and can significantly enhance customer satisfaction. Ensuring that you have a robust strategy for maintenance contracts, warranties and guarantees, and follow-up services will set you apart from the competition and help you build lasting relationships with your clients.

Maintenance Contracts

Stepping into the world of electrical services, one of the most reliable ways to ensure ongoing customer satisfaction while stabilising your income is to offer maintenance contracts. Think of these contracts not just as a business agreement, but as an ongoing relationship between you and your client. They are about ensuring that the electrical systems you work on continue to operate efficiently, safely, and effectively long after your initial job is completed.

Maintenance contracts can vary widely, but typically, they involve regular inspections, the testing of electrical systems, and the preventative maintenance of equipment and circuits. The frequency and scope of these services often depend on the complexity of the system and the operational requirements of the client's business or home.

From your perspective as a newly qualified electrician, offering maintenance contracts provides a predictable revenue stream—a safety net that can help you through slower periods. More importantly, these contracts put you in regular contact with your clients, building trust and positioning you as their go-to expert in electrical matters.

Here's how to get started: Begin by outlining what your maintenance contract will cover. Will you offer monthly check-ups, or is a quarterly visit sufficient? What specific services will you include? Will there be different tiers or levels of service? Once you've defined the scope, make sure your pricing is competitive yet reflective of the value you provide. Remember, clarity is key—both you and your client should understand what is covered under the contract to avoid any future disputes.

Warranty and Guarantees

Warranties and guarantees are your promise to your client that the work you perform is reliable and of high quality. They serve as your client's safety net, providing peace of mind that they won't face immediate additional costs if something goes wrong due to workmanship or materials that are below standard.

As a newly qualified electrician, offering a solid warranty can significantly enhance your reputation. It shows that you stand behind your work and are confident in your skills. But be careful—your warranty should be sustainable for your business. Clearly define what your warranty covers and, equally important, what it does not cover. This might include limitations on time (e.g., a one-year warranty on installation) or specific exclusions (e.g., damage caused by external factors like weather or unauthorised modifications by third parties).

Communicate your warranty terms clearly at the outset. This transparency helps manage customer expectations and reduces the likelihood of misunderstandings. Should a situation arise where a client claims under warranty, handle it promptly and professionally. This not only resolves the immediate issue but also reinforces your reputation as a reliable and honourable professional.

Follow-Up Services

Last but certainly not least, let's talk about follow-up services. Following up might seem like a small part of the process, but it's a powerful tool for building long-lasting customer relationships. A simple follow-up call or email after a job can make your client feel valued and cared for. It shows that you are not just about making a quick profit but are genuinely interested in their safety and satisfaction.

Implement a systematic approach to following up. Schedule a call or send an email a few weeks after completing a job to ask if everything is working as it should and if they have any concerns or further needs. This not only gives you the chance to address any small issues before they become big problems, but it also keeps you fresh in the client's mind for future electrical needs or referrals.

Moreover, follow-up services can sometimes lead to additional work. During these interactions, clients might mention other areas in their home or business that could benefit from your expertise. Always be ready to discuss how you can help, perhaps by offering a brief free consultation as part of your follow-up process.

In conclusion, aftercare services are not just about maintaining electrical systems; they're about maintaining relationships. By implementing robust maintenance contracts, offering clear and fair warranties and guarantees, and providing thoughtful follow-up services, you not only ensure customer satisfaction but also pave the way for a flourishing career in the electrical industry. Remember, each client interaction is a stepping stone to another, potentially larger opportunity. Treat it as such, and watch your business grow.

Recap & Action Items

Alright, you've just powered through a crucial chapter on Ensuring Customer Satisfaction. Let's boil it down: It's all about delivering quality, handling feedback constructively, and offering stellar aftercare. These aren't just tasks; they're your stepping stones to building a reputable career in the electrical field.

First off, focus on quality workmanship. This is your foundation. Always align with the latest standards and compliance requirements—it's non-negotiable. Implement thorough quality control processes in your daily work and be diligent about handling revisions and corrections. Remember, excellence in your work is a massive part of why clients will trust and recommend you.

Next up, feedback. Embrace it. Encourage your customers to share their thoughts and feelings about your service. When complaints come—and they will—respond professionally and see them as opportunities to improve and innovate. Every piece of feedback is valuable, even when it stings a bit. Use it to refine your skills and services.

Lastly, don't forget the aftercare. Offering maintenance contracts, warranties, and follow-ups isn't just good business sense—it shows your clients that you care about the longevity and reliability of your work. This kind of commitment can set you apart from the pack.

Here's what you can start doing right away:

1. Create a checklist for compliance and quality control that you can follow for each job

2. Set up a simple feedback system, perhaps starting with follow-up calls or feedback forms

3. Develop a template for responding to customer complaints that helps you reply promptly and constructively

4. Outline the terms of aftercare you want to provide and make sure they're clearly communicated to your clients.

Implement these steps, and you'll not only meet customer expectations; you'll exceed them. And in a profession like yours, exceeding expectations can mean the difference between a one-time job and a lifelong client. Remember, in the vast network of wires and circuits that power our world, your commitment to customer satisfaction is the true connector.

Building a Strong Professional Network

"Your network is your net worth." - *Porter Gale*

Networking Strategies

Embarking on your career as a newly qualified electrician, you might find the electrical world buzzing with more than just currents and circuits; it's alive with opportunities for those who connect the right wires in the networking sphere. Much like ensuring a solid wiring system, building a robust professional network can dramatically influence your career trajectory. Let's break down some effective strategies that can amplify your professional connections.

Industry Associations and Groups

First up, let's talk about industry associations and groups. Think of these as the circuit breakers in your networking system—they can prevent overloads and ensure everything runs smoothly. Joining a professional association is akin to plugging into a powerful source of knowledge, resources, and connections.

For electricians in the UK, organisations such as the Electrical Contractors' Association (ECA) or the Independent Electrical Contractors (IEC) serve as excellent starting points. These groups offer a platform not only to meet peers but also to stay abreast of industry standards, regulations, and innovations. Membership often provides access to exclusive training sessions, certification courses, and newsletters that keep you updated on the latest in electrical technology and business practices.

Participation goes beyond mere membership; it's about engagement. Attend meetings, volunteer for committees, or even present at events. Each interaction increases your visibility in the industry and opens up new avenues for professional growth. Remember, the more active you are, the more beneficial your memberships will be. It's not just about having the logo on your resume; it's about making genuine connections that could lead to job offers, partnerships, or valuable mentorships.

Attending Trade Shows and Conferences

Next on the agenda is harnessing the power of trade shows and conferences. These events are like live circuits, buzzing with energy and potential. They provide a unique convergence of professionals, from novices to experts, all under one roof, discussing trends, technology, and techniques that are shaping the future of electrical engineering.

Before attending any trade show or conference, do your homework. Identify the events that are most relevant to your interests and career goals. Whether it's a local trade fair focusing on sustainable energy solutions or an international conference showcasing cutting-edge electrical systems, choose wisely to make the most of your time and investment.

Once you're there, engage actively. Participate in workshops, attend keynote speeches, and don't shy away from Q&A sessions. These interactions are not just learning opportunities; they're a chance to ask questions and express thoughts to thought leaders and innovators in your field. And let's not forget the exhibition stands—often overlooked, these are goldmines for starting conversations with established companies and startups alike.

Networking in these settings is about quality, not just quantity. It's better to have five meaningful conversations than to leave with a stack of business cards you'll never use. When you connect with someone, follow up—a quick LinkedIn message or an email can help turn a brief encounter at a conference into a lasting professional relationship.

Online Professional Networks

In today's digital age, online professional networks are indispensable tools for building and maintaining connections.

Platforms like LinkedIn are not just online resumes; they are dynamic ecosystems where you can engage with a global network of professionals.

Start by crafting a compelling profile that highlights your qualifications, projects, and professional interests. Use a professional photo, write a clear, concise bio, and don't hesitate to showcase your achievements and certifications. Think of your LinkedIn profile as your digital handshake—it needs to be strong and confident.

But networking online goes beyond setting up a profile. Join groups and forums that are relevant to electricians. Engage in discussions, share articles, and comment on posts. By contributing valuable insights, you establish yourself as an active and knowledgeable member of the community. These platforms also frequently host virtual events and webinars, offering additional opportunities to learn and network without the need to travel.

Moreover, consider the broader implications of your online presence. Your interactions and the content you share contribute to your professional brand. Always be mindful of the image you're projecting. A respectful, informed, and proactive online persona can open doors to opportunities that traditional networking might miss.

By weaving together these strands—industry associations, trade shows, and online networks—you create a strong and resilient networking grid. Each element compliments the others, providing a comprehensive approach to building professional relationships. As you step forward in your career, remember that networking is about mutual benefit. The connections you make are not just for your own advancement—they're about sharing knowledge, experiences, and opportunities. The more you invest in these relationships, the more you and your career will thrive in the electrifying field of electrical engineering.

Mentorship and Collaboration

Mentorship and collaboration are integral to personal and professional development, offering opportunities for shared knowledge and cooperative efforts. This sub-chapter explores essential aspects, including finding mentors, engaging in collaborative projects, and participating actively in community initiatives. These elements are crucial for nurturing skills, expanding networks, and making meaningful contributions in diverse environments.

Finding a Mentor

Embarking on your career as a newly qualified electrician, you might often find yourself in scenarios where practical advice seems as necessary as a trusty wire stripper. That's where a mentor comes into play. A mentor is not just someone who teaches you the ropes; they are your industry guide, career advocate, and sometimes, your emergency contact when things go sideways on a complex job.

Finding the right mentor involves identifying someone whose career path aligns somewhat with where you envision your own journey heading. Start by scoping out your immediate professional circle—this could be a more experienced colleague at your current job or an industry professional you've met at events. Don't shy away from reaching out; most experienced professionals are flattered by the request and keen to share their knowledge.

Another effective strategy is to utilise online platforms such as LinkedIn. Join electrician groups and participate in discussions. Once you've identified a potential mentor there, engage with their posts and share your thoughts respectfully. After establishing a rapport, a well-crafted, polite message explaining your career aspirations and requesting mentorship can go a long way.

Remember, the relationship with your mentor should be reciprocal. Yes, your mentor provides guidance, but always think about how you can bring value to their life as well, be it through assisting with projects, sharing insights on the latest industry tech, or even volunteering for tasks they need help with.

Collaborative Projects

Engaging in collaborative projects is like the live-wiring of your career—it's where theory meets practice, and ideas spark into reality. Collaborations allow you to blend your skills with others, often leading to innovative solutions and learning opportunities that you might not encounter if working solo.

Look for opportunities within your workplace to join or initiate projects that involve teamwork. It could be as simple as offering to assist a senior electrician on a complex installation or volunteering for a community project that needs electrical expertise. Each project is a chance to observe different work styles and techniques, which is invaluable as you refine your own approach.

Beyond the workplace, consider joining or forming a study group with fellow electricians. These groups can focus on different aspects, from technical updates in the electrical field to business skills like managing contracts and client communications. Participating in such groups can enhance your understanding and provide a support system as you navigate your career.

Local trade schools or community colleges often host hackathons or project contests that can also serve as excellent platforms for collaborative experiences. These events not only bolster your CV but also put you in the same room with potential mentors, peers, and even future business partners.

Community Involvement

Community involvement is a brilliant strategy not just for personal growth but also for strengthening your professional network. It positions you as a proactive, involved, and reliable individual within your local area—a great reputation to have, especially in a field like electrical work where trust and reliability are paramount.

Start with local community centres or non-profits that might benefit from your skills. Offering to fix wiring or install new fixtures can make a significant difference in these settings and introduce you to a network of people who could turn into clients or recommend your services to others.

Participating in community safety programmes is another avenue. You could volunteer to give talks on electrical safety, which not only helps in preventing accidents but also establishes you as an authority figure in the electrical field within your community.

For broader impact, align with national or global initiatives that focus on energy conservation and sustainable practices. Initiatives such as these not only provide networking opportunities but also align you with the future direction of the industry, which is increasingly leaning towards sustainable practices.

Through these channels of mentorship, collaboration, and community involvement, you are not just building a network; you are setting the foundation for a robust, dynamic, and fulfilling career. Each interaction is a thread in the larger fabric of your professional life, and how you choose to weave these threads will define the strength and resilience of your career path. Continue to reach out, engage, and participate. Your future as a successful electrician depends not just on your skills with the tools, but equally on your ability to connect, collaborate, and lead in the community around you.

Reputation Management

Reputation Management is a critical aspect of maintaining trust and credibility in any professional or personal endeavor. This section delves into strategies and practices essential for safeguarding and enhancing one's reputation. By understanding and implementing effective reputation management techniques, individuals and organizations can navigate challenges, build resilience, and cultivate a positive public perception.

Online Reviews and Testimonials

In the digital age, your online reputation can be your strongest asset or your biggest liability. As a newly qualified electrician, it's essential to harness the power of online reviews and testimonials. Think of each positive review as a stepping stone towards your next big job or project. But how do you get these glowing recommendations?

Firstly, always provide exceptional service. This goes beyond fixing the problem at hand; it includes being punctual, polite, and professional. After you've completed a job, don't hesitate to ask your satisfied customers to leave a review on popular platforms like Google, Trustpilot, or even directly on your business website. Most customers are happy to share their positive experiences if they feel they've received value.

Moreover, make it easy for them. Send a follow-up email with direct links to your review profiles. You can even create a simple instructional guide on how to leave a review, which can help those who might not be as tech-savvy.

Handling negative reviews is also part of the game. Don't ignore them—address them promptly and professionally. Apologise if necessary, and offer to correct any issues. This not only potentially salvages a professional relationship but also shows prospective clients that you're committed to customer satisfaction. Remember, a well-handled negative review can sometimes be as influential as a positive one!

Dealing with Negative Publicity

No matter how proficient you are, negative publicity can occur, and it's crucial to handle it with grace. If you find yourself the subject of unfavourable news or social media attention, take a proactive stance. Assess the situation carefully—sometimes what seems disastrous can actually be a minor hiccup if managed correctly.

Always respond rather than react. This means taking the time to understand the complaint or issue fully before crafting your public response. Transparency is key; acknowledge the problem and outline the steps you will take to resolve it. This approach not only helps in mitigating the damage but also in rebuilding trust.

If the issue is complex, don't shy away from seeking professional help. Public relations specialists can provide invaluable advice on navigating through stormy waters. They can help you draft responses, manage social media fallout, and even reframe the issue to highlight your commitment to improvement and professionalism.

Maintaining a calm and professional demeanour during such times can turn a potentially career-damaging situation into a testament to your resilience and dedication to your craft.

Personal Branding

As a newly established electrician, crafting your personal brand goes beyond mere logos and business cards. It's about presenting yourself consistently, online and offline, while effectively communicating your values and expertise.

Begin by identifying what sets you apart. Whether it's your dedication to sustainable practices, innovative problem-solving skills, or exceptional customer service, highlight these strengths consistently across all your marketing efforts.

Develop a professional website that showcases your skills, previous projects, and client testimonials. Utilize social media platforms to share valuable content related to electrical work, such as energy-saving tips or updates on industry advancements. This not only reinforces your expertise but also maintains engagement with your audience and peers.

Consider contributing articles or blogs on topics relevant to your field. This approach not only boosts your visibility on search engines but also positions you as a trusted authority within the industry. Platforms like LinkedIn provide an ideal space to publish professional insights that enhance your credibility and attract targeted attention.

Networking is equally vital for shaping your personal brand. Attend industry events, workshops, and seminars to connect with fellow professionals. Engaging in these interactions isn't just about potential job opportunities but also about sharing knowledge and experiences. The relationships you cultivate will significantly impact your personal brand, bolstering your reputation in the field.

Remember, every interaction presents an opportunity to strengthen your brand. Whether it's how you handle client calls, your conduct on the job site, or your responsiveness to emails, consistent professionalism will steadily build a robust and positive reputation over time.

By focusing on these three key areas of reputation management, you can ensure that your career as an electrician starts on the right foot and continues to grow in a positive direction. Remember, your reputation is like a shadow—always there, reflecting your professional journey. Make it count.

Recap & Action Items

Congratulations! You've just equipped yourself with a robust set of strategies to build a strong professional network, a pivotal step in your journey as an electrician. Let's quickly recap the pillars we've covered: networking strategies, mentorship and collaboration, and reputation management. Each of these are crucial for not just surviving, but thriving in the electrical industry.

Now, what's next? It's time to transform this knowledge into action. Here's what you can do:

1. **Join Industry Associations and Groups**: Dive in and become an active member. Don't just be a name on a membership list. Engage, attend meetings, volunteer for committees. This isn't just about showing up; it's about being involved and making genuine connections.

2. **Attend Trade Shows and Conferences**: Mark your calendar with relevant events and prepare to make the most out of them. Have your questions ready, bring your business cards, and don't shy away from initiating conversations. Remember, the more you put into these experiences, the more you'll get out.

3. **Harness Online Professional Networks**: Create a standout profile on platforms like LinkedIn. Connect with both new contacts and seasoned professionals. Share insights, join discussions, and showcase your projects or achievements.

4. **Seek Out a Mentor**: Identify someone whose career path aligns with your aspirations. Reach out for guidance, be respectful of their time, and demonstrate your eagerness to learn. This relationship can be a game-changer for your career.

5. **Engage in Collaborative Projects**: Whether it's within your company or through community initiatives, look for opportunities to collaborate. These projects are not just about the technical skills; they're about teamwork, problem-solving, and leadership.

6. **Boost Your Community Involvement**: Get involved in local community projects or offer workshops. This builds your network, enhances your reputation, and contributes positively to your locality.

7. **Manage Your Online Reputation**: Encourage satisfied clients to leave positive reviews and tactfully address any negative feedback. Regularly update your digital footprint to reflect the professional you are.

8. **Develop Your Personal Brand**: Think about what sets you apart and how you want to be perceived in the industry. Your personal brand is your career's signature and should resonate with your professional ethos and style.

Each step you take builds upon the last, creating a compounding effect that enhances your professional standing and opens up new opportunities. Networking isn't just about collecting contacts; it's about cultivating relationships that are mutually beneficial. Remember, every interaction is a chance to learn, grow, and contribute to your field. So, get out there, connect, collaborate, and create the career you've always wanted.

Planning for the Future

"Someone's sitting in the shade today because someone planted a tree a long time ago." – Warren Buffett

Scaling Your Business

So, you've nailed down the basics of being an electrician, and your business is sparking interest and drawing clients. But what's next? How do you turn your solo venture into a powerhouse that not only survives but thrives in the competitive market? Let's dive into some strategies that can help you scale your business effectively.

When to Hire Employees

Scaling a business often means you can't go it alone anymore. Hiring your first employee is a significant step, symbolising your transition from a self-employed technician to a business owner. The**Scaling Your Business**

Embarking on the journey of scaling your business as a newly qualified electrician can be as thrilling as it is daunting. But fear not! With the right strategies and insights, you can elevate your fledgling enterprise to new heights. Let's break down the crucial steps: hiring employees, training and managing your team, and expanding geographically.

When to Hire Employees

Knowing when to hire employees is pivotal. It's about striking a balance between growing demand and sustainable expansion. Initially, you might be handling all tasks yourself, from client consultations to the actual electrical work and everything in between. However, keep a keen eye on certain signs that suggest it's time to expand your team.

Firstly, monitor your workload. If you find yourself consistently working late nights or turning down projects because you're stretched too thin, it's a signal to consider hiring. Moreover, expanding your workforce isn't merely about alleviating workload; it's also about enhancing your business's capabilities and service quality.

Secondly, assess your financial health. Expanding your team means additional expenses, not just in salaries but also in tools, training, and possibly more workspace. Ensure you have a steady flow of income and some savings to cushion the initial financial impact of hiring.

Lastly, listen to your customers. Feedback often includes invaluable insights into how your business can improve and grow. If clients are requesting services or faster completion times you currently can't deliver solo, it might be time to bring more hands on deck.

Training and Managing a Team

Once you've decided to hire, the next step is ensuring your team is well-trained and effectively managed. Remember, the quality of work your team produces can make or break your reputation.

Start by setting clear, achievable expectations. During training, focus on the skills that are crucial to your business's operations. It's not just about technical skills—emphasize the importance of customer service, which is often as important as technical expertise in building customer loyalty and satisfaction.

Adopting a mentoring approach can be tremendously effective. Pair newly hired electricians with more experienced ones. This not only helps in transferring knowledge but also sets a collaborative tone within your team. Regular feedback and open communication channels are key in fostering a positive work environment and addressing any issues proactively.

Management isn't just about overseeing; it's about leading by example. Show commitment, integrity, and respect - qualities that inspire and motivate. Utilize tools and software to streamline scheduling, job tracking, and customer management to keep your business operations smooth and responsive.

Expanding Geographically

Expanding your business geographically can be an exciting step towards broadening your market reach and client base. However, this move should be calculated and strategic.

First, research potential new markets. Look for areas with growing housing markets, commercial development, or insufficient electrical services. Understand the local regulations and licensing requirements, as these can vary significantly.

Secondly, start small. Before committing to opening a new branch, test the waters with targeted marketing campaigns or temporary service offers in the desired area. This can provide valuable insights into the local market demand without the full commitment of opening a new location.

Building local partnerships can be a game changer. Connect with local contractors, real estate developers, and other service providers. These relationships can lead to referrals and joint ventures that might be crucial in establishing your presence in a new area.

Lastly, keep your original business base strong while you expand. It's essential to maintain the quality and reliability of your service in your established area even as you reach out to new markets. Neglecting your initial customer base can lead to a decrease in overall business health.

Scaling your business is not without its challenges, but with thoughtful planning and execution, it can lead to rewarding growth and success. Remember, every big venture started small, and every industry leader began with a single step. So, harness your skills, learn continuously, and push forward with confidence. Your electrician's blueprint isn't just about wires and circuits; it's about building a robust, thriving business that lights up not just homes but also your life.

Innovations and Trends

In the field of electrical engineering, staying ahead involves anticipating future directions and embracing change. This sub-chapter explores crucial elements: Future Trends in Electrical Engineering, where emerging technologies and advancements are scrutinized for their potential impact. Investing strategically delves into the importance of research and development, fostering solutions that drive industry leadership. Additionally, Preparing for Market Changes underscores proactive strategies to anticipate and adapt to evolving demands, ensuring continued relevance and competitive edge in the dynamic landscape of electrical engineering.

Future Trends in Electrical Engineering

As you begin to carve out your niche in the electrical industry, staying ahead of the curve is crucial. The sector is evolving rapidly, influenced by technological advancements and societal shifts towards sustainability. One of the most significant trends you should be aware of is the integration of smart technology in homes and businesses. Smart systems are being designed to enhance energy efficiency and user convenience, which means a growing demand for electricians who can install and manage these systems.

Moreover, renewable energy sources such as solar panels and wind turbines are becoming more prevalent. As these technologies become more accessible, your expertise in installing and maintaining such systems will be invaluable. Additionally, the rise of electric vehicles (EVs) is creating a new avenue for electrical professionals. EV charging stations are popping up everywhere, from residential garages to commercial car parks, and they require skilled electricians to install and maintain them.

Lastly, consider the advancements in lighting technology, particularly LED and OLED technologies, which not only reduce energy consumption but also offer longer lifespans than traditional lighting systems. These technologies are not just trends; they are the future, and understanding them now could position you as a specialist in a lucrative niche.

Investing in Innovation

Investing in your continuous professional development by learning about new technologies and innovations in the electrical field is not just beneficial; it's essential. It keeps your skills relevant and competitive in a market that values technological proficiency and innovative solutions.

Start by dedicating time to learning. This could be through online courses, workshops, or seminars focused on the latest electrical technologies and practices. Manufacturers often offer training sessions on new products, which can be a great way to stay updated while also networking with other professionals in your field.

Another way to invest in innovation is by upgrading your tools and equipment. For instance, thermal imaging cameras can help you diagnose issues without invasive measures, saving time and increasing client satisfaction. Similarly, investing in more sophisticated testing and diagnostic tools can enhance your ability to troubleshoot complex problems quickly and effectively.

Remember, investing in innovation also means embracing software and apps designed to streamline your business operations. From project management tools to invoicing and scheduling apps, leveraging these technologies can free up your time so you can focus more on strategic tasks and less on administrative chores.

Preparing for Market Changes

The electrical industry, like many others, is subject to shifts caused by economic changes, regulatory updates, and technological advancements. Preparing for these changes is not just about survival; it's about thriving in a transforming landscape.

Firstly, keep abreast of regulatory changes. Government regulations can have a profound impact on how electrical work is carried out. Whether it's new safety standards or changes in licensing requirements, being informed will ensure you remain compliant and avoid potential legal issues.

Secondly, monitor economic trends. Economic downturns can lead to reduced demand for new installations but might increase demand for repair and maintenance services. Conversely, an economic boom could result in an influx of new construction projects requiring electrical expertise. By understanding these cycles, you can adjust your business strategy to maintain steady growth.

Lastly, listen to your customers. They are often your best source of information when it comes to shifting preferences and needs. For instance, if you notice an increase in requests for energy-efficient installations, it might be time to consider specialising in eco-friendly electrical solutions.

By staying informed about future trends, investing wisely in innovation, and preparing for market changes, you can ensure that your electrical career not only survives but thrives in the coming years. Keep learning, stay adaptable, and always look ahead to anticipate what's next on the horizon.

Exit Strategies

An essential consideration for any electrical business owner is your exit strategy, whether preparing for sale or succession. This section delves into critical areas such as Valuation of an Electrical Business, where understanding the worth of your enterprise is pivotal for informed decisions. Additionally, Retirement Planning is explored to ensure a smooth transition, safeguarding personal financial security and the legacy of the business. By addressing these facets thoughtfully, owners can navigate transitions with clarity and confidence, ensuring the continuity and success of their endeavors.

Preparing for Sale or Succession

As you navigate through your career as an electrician, there will come a time when you start thinking about either selling your business or passing it on to a successor. This is not just about cashing in chips; it's a strategic move that safeguards your financial future and ensures the continuity of your business.

First off, understanding the right time to initiate this process is crucial. Ideally, you don't want to start planning your exit when you're desperate to step down or when the business is in a decline. Begin when the business is thriving, as this not only increases its valuation but also makes it more attractive to potential buyers or successors.

Next, get your business evaluated by a professional. This not only gives you a clear picture of where your business stands but also helps in pinpointing areas that could improve your company's value before you sell or hand it over. Consider factors like your client base, your business model, ongoing contracts, and the robustness of your financial systems.

Documentation is your best friend here. Ensure all your business processes, client contracts, and financial records are well-documented and up to date. These elements are crucial for a smooth transition. They also provide transparency and trust, qualities that potential buyers or successors deeply value.

Lastly, think about whether you want to sell outright or gradually transition out of your role. If you opt for the latter, you might consider bringing in a partner or gradually transferring responsibilities and ownership to an existing employee or family member, ensuring a seamless succession.

Valuation of an Electrical Business

Valuing an electrical business is more art than science. It involves not just looking at numbers but understanding what those numbers represent. Potential buyers or successors will scrutinise everything: from your annual turnover to client satisfaction rates, from the scalability of your business model to the stability of your earnings.

There are several methods to consider when valuing your business. The 'Earnings Multiplier' approach is often used, where your business's net profit is multiplied by an industry-standard figure. Alternatively, the 'Asset-Based' approach focuses on the tangible and intangible assets owned by the business. However, for service-oriented businesses like electrical services, the 'Discounted Cash Flow' method can be more appropriate. This method forecasts your business's future cash flows and discounts them to present value, providing a picture of your business's potential worth.

It's also essential to factor in 'goodwill', which represents the value of your business's reputation and customer relationships. This can often be the most significant part of an electrical business's valuation, particularly if you have established a strong brand and loyal customer base.

Engage with a professional business valuator or an accountant who understands the intricacies of your industry. They can provide a realistic and fair valuation, giving you a solid foundation for negotiations with potential buyers or planning for succession.

Retirement Planning

Planning for retirement is about preparing for the day when you no longer need to work to sustain your lifestyle. For electricians, who often deal with physical tasks, planning might need to start earlier than in other professions. Pensions, savings, investments, and other income streams need to be considered to ensure a comfortable retirement.

Start by looking at your pension options. If you're self-employed, setting up a personal pension like a Self-Invested Personal Pension (SIPP) or a stakeholder pension is vital. These allow you to control where your money is invested and benefit from tax relief.

Diversifying your income is also crucial. Consider investing in assets that can generate passive income, such as real estate or stocks. This diversification not only spreads risk but also provides you with a safety net, should one income stream dry up.

Additionally, explore ways to keep your skills relevant and consider consultancy or part-time roles in the future. This can not only supplement your pension but also keep you engaged and mentally active.

Finally, don't overlook the value of a clear financial plan. Work with a financial advisor to map out your retirement goals and the steps needed to achieve them. Review this plan regularly to adapt to any changes in your circumstances or goals.

Navigating the path to selling your business, valuating it accurately, and planning for a financially secure retirement are all crucial components of your exit strategy. Each step should be taken with careful thought and planning. Engaging with professionals who can guide and advise you through this process is invaluable. Remember, the decisions you make today will shape not just your future but also the legacy of your electrical career.

Recap & Action Items

Congratulations! You've just navigated through some crucial strategies to ensure not just the growth but the sustained success of your electrical business. Now, let's cement those insights with practical steps you can take right away.

Firstly, think about scaling your business. It's time to assess your current workload and future projects. If you're consistently overbooked and turning down opportunities, it might be the perfect moment to consider hiring. Start small with one or two employees and focus on roles that will free up your time for more complex tasks or allow you to accept more work. Remember, effective training and management are key. Invest in a simple, yet comprehensive training programme to ensure your team can meet your standards of quality and efficiency.

Next, keep your eyes on the future of the industry. Stay abreast of trends such as renewable energy technologies, smart home installations, and sustainability practices. Consider allocating a portion of your profits to attend workshops or courses that focus on these innovations. This knowledge not only sets you apart from the competition but can also open new avenues for business growth.

Finally, it's never too early to think about an exit strategy. Whether you plan to sell your business, pass it on to a family member, or simply retire comfortably, planning is essential. Start by understanding the value of your business. Engage with a financial advisor who specialises in your industry to help estimate the worth of your business and guide you through the process of increasing its value over time.

As you implement these steps, maintain a balance between immediate actions and long-term planning. Keep revisiting your goals, adjusting as necessary, and always strive for improvement. Your journey as an electrician is not just about the wires and circuits; it's about building a thriving, resilient business that lights up the future, both for yourself and the community you serve.

Shaping Your Electrical Future

As you turn the pages of this guide, each chapter has strategically paved a road from the fundamentals to the sophisticated nuances of a career that thrives on the very current that powers our world—electricity. Now, as you stand at the precipice of this journey, ready to harness the full potential of your skills and ambitions, it's crucial to reflect on what lies ahead and how you can mould your path to success.

Success in the electrician's field, much like in any trade, isn't just about skill—it's equally about strategy, perseverance, and the continuous pursuit of growth. You've learnt how to land your first job and leap into self-employment; you've explored ways to expand your client base and ventured through the intricacies of mastering the business side of electricity. Each of these steps was a building block, not just in your career but in crafting the entrepreneur within you.

Now, imagine a future where you are not just a participant in the electrical industry but a defining force. Envision employing innovative solutions that enhance efficiency and safety, pushing the boundaries of what is possible within your field. The road doesn't end here; it merely escalates to new challenges and opportunities. It's about taking everything you have learnt and mixing it with an unyielding drive to innovate and lead. This is where you transform from a professional into a visionary.

In an era where technology evolves at an unprecedented pace, the demand for skilled electricians who are not only technically proficient but also capable of critical thinking and adaptation is soaring. The landscape of the electrical trade is shifting, with a growing emphasis on sustainable and smart technologies. This shift isn't just a challenge; it's an array of opportunities—an opportunity to be at the forefront of ecological and technological advancements, an opportunity to lead projects that not only light up homes but also pave the way for a greener planet.

However, embracing these opportunities requires more than just technical know-how. It calls for an entrepreneurial spirit, a knack for understanding market needs, and an unquenchable thirst for learning. It demands resilience in the face of setbacks and the courage to step outside comfort zones. Whether it's adopting new technologies, expanding into new markets, or creating more efficient business models, the future belongs to those who are prepared to innovate and adapt.

But what does it take to not just survive but thrive in this evolving landscape? It takes continuous learning and personal development. It takes networking with other professionals who can offer insights and support that you might not have considered. It takes a willingness to invest in yourself and your business, ensuring that both can adapt and grow in a changing environment. And most importantly, it takes a clear vision of your goals and the persistence to achieve them.

If you're ready to take that next step and are seeking guidance tailored specifically to your unique situation, remember, professional help is just a reach away. Whether you need assistance in scaling your business, advice on the latest technologies, or strategies to enhance customer satisfaction, help is available. Visit **www.pdelectrical.info** to explore how personalised counsel can propel you towards your goals.

This is your moment to shine brighter than ever, to electrify your future and energise your career. Do not hesitate to reach out and grasp the future that awaits. The path has been set, the tools provided and now, the journey ahead is yours to command. Let your actions define your legacy in the electric world.

Remember, every great achievement begins with the decision to try. Trust in your skills, leverage your knowledge, and continuously seek out the expertise that will enable you to soar. With each step forward, you are not just building circuits; you are building a future—your future.

So, take a deep breath, and let's power up this journey. Your electric future isn't just about maintaining the flow; it's about creating sparks that ignite innovation and lead change.

Are you ready to switch on your potential? Visit **www.pdelectrical.info** today, and let's illuminate the possibilities together. Your future is bright, charged, and waiting. Let's make it electrifying.

www.ingramcontent.com/pod-product-compliance
Lightning Source LLC
Chambersburg PA
CBHW071830210526
45479CB00001B/76